HOW TO DISAPPEAR

HOW TO
DISAPPEAR

a memoir for misfits

Duncan Fallowell

TERRACE BOOKS

A TRADE IMPRINT OF THE UNIVERSITY OF WISCONSIN PRESS

Terrace Books
A trade imprint of the University of Wisconsin Press
1930 Monroe Street, 3rd Floor
Madison, Wisconsin 53711-2059
uwpress.wisc.edu

Printed in the United States of America

Library of Congress Cataloging-in-Publication Data

Fallowell, Duncan.
How to disappear : a memoir for misfits / Duncan Fallowell.
p.   cm.
Originally published: London : Ditto Press, 2011.
ISBN 978-0-299-29240-9 (cloth : alk. paper)
ISBN 978-0-299-29243-0 (e-book)
1. Fallowell, Duncan—Travel. I. Title.
PR6056.A56Z46   2013
823'.914—dc23
[B]
2012040153

Typeset in Plantin Rounded

To my old friend Pedro Friedeberg
whom I've never met

Contents

How to Disappear

CHAPTER ONE

Sailing to Gozo

We are held for two days in Catania port by storms of unusual violence, and all Mount Aetna and much of the town have disappeared in a turbulence of drenching cloud. Lit by lightning, a baroque dome or a line of statues or a towerblock might briefly flash out at an unexpected angle; but thunder can barely be heard above the roar of winds whose force whips the rain into diagonals, stinging the face on deck or blasting smears against the portholes when we're inside. Our ship has the protection of the basin, but immense waves, so uncharacteristic of the Mediterranean, break against the far side of the harbour wall, sending displays of foam up to a great height. These sudden bouquets of whiteness are snatched by the gales and are dispersed into the maelstrom, so that the sea seems to explode and vanish upwards.

Ever phlegmatic, the crew play cards in the saloon while the passengers, few at this time of year (only a couple of dozen on a ship which could take hundreds as well as their automobiles), stare out with listless eyes at the dim chaos. Occasionally someone dashes down the gangplank, along the harbourside and into town, to buy the chewy almond cakes for which Catania is famous. In due course he will reappear, sodden but triumphant, with a bow-tied parcel in a dripping plastic bag. The cakes, not too sweet yet dusted in a talcum of sugar, are tenderly satisfying, especially when taken with tea. Alas, the tea on offer at the ship's bar is without doubt the most repulsive I've ever come across, its taste a mixture of filth and antiseptic, its colour a perturbed grey. And the coffee's not much better.

On the third morning one awakes to peace. All violence has departed and the city, beneath a blue sky, is meticulously exposed by sunlight of butter-yellow. Somewhat darker and behind it, but not forbidding, Aetna slides gracefully to the heavens; while during breakfast on board nobody speaks, everyone muted by tranquillity or tedium. The gluelike hours move slowly forward until at last, after half an hour of premonitory throbbing and squirting through its flanks, the ship sets sail for Malta at I pm.

We hug the Sicilian coast, cruising southwards. Squinting passengers take the air on deck. Unexpectedly, blocks of flats appear on the shore, followed by the cluster of old Syracuse which is our only stopping point before the open sea. At the very mention of 'Syracuse' an enchantment arises in one's mind: palace and opera house, cathedral and café, ancient gold stone and young gold flesh, palm fronds, handbag snatchers, wonderful food alfresco on warm velvet nights, and death in carnival costume; all the heady and crooked clichés of the south jostling softly together–the locus of another story–not this one.

The ship, in the smartly painted blue-and-white of the Tirrenia Line, is an unavoidable spectacle when it ties up alongside the esplanade. This is known as the Foro Italico and is marked out by a string of pom-pom trees overlooked by a precipice of grand houses. Scootering children greet our arrival, then stand dumbly and stare up at the floating bulk while seven more passengers join the ship. Four of them, bent by heavy bags of foodstuffs, turn out to be residents of Gozo and are English.

'Is Gozo like Sicily?' I ask.

'Not in the slightest. Sicily is civilisation.'

Really? At times in Sicily I have felt far from the security of the word 'civilisation' whose very syllables rumble so elegantly along like the roofscape of a classical ideal; and I've found myself instead in a place where I could not walk or talk freely and where at any moment I might be ambushed. When Coleridge came up to Syracuse from Valletta around 1805 he also had mixed feelings. Syracuse he found decayed and the population deep in ignorance, swarmed over by Catholic priests as numerous, he wrote, as an Egyptian plague. But, as always in Sicily, there was voluptuousness too: at the opera, he noted, and in the cakey palazzi, and in the fertile spaces between ancient ruins where, to Coleridge's surprise, Indian hemp and the opium poppy grew happily and were harvested by the Syracusans for their narcotic properties. Which was right up his street, for not only was Coleridge addicted to laudanum but I read somewhere that he invented a cocktail consisting of aconite, angostura, and leopard's bane.

'Where will you be staying?' asks one of the Englishmen.

'I fancied the sound of the Duke of Edinburgh.' This hotel is in Victoria, Gozo's capital.

'Ah...' comes the response.

'What do you mean, "ah"?'

'Do you like character?'

'Yes.'

'Then you'll love it.'

'I haven't booked or anything.'

'At this time of the year it will be empty.'

He turns back to his companions, leaving me to purse my lips and look at nothing, swimming a little inside, which I recognise as the careen of the unknown, of a dubious situation up ahead which is to be faced alone. It is succeeded by a short, corrective burst of adrenaline.

We sail south-south-west. Everything is fine for an hour and a half or so – then without warning the ship slides down a steep bank of water into a lurching swell. At first it is almost amusing, in funfair fashion, but one by one the passengers turn avocado-green and disappear into their cabins. On deck a pregnant woman collapses in disorientation. With her legs buckling this way and that, head lolling and eyes rolling as though in the final throes of mad cow disease (her ballooning cargo of unborn flesh threatening to take off in yet another direction), she is helped below by companions.

Usually I do not suffer from sea-sickness beyond a slightly queasy sense of surprise. I do what one is supposed to do: use the horizon to maintain at least one constant in a world of liquefying references. But eventually I too begin to feel uncomfortable and decide to go below for something to settle the stomach. On the way I pass a splattered mess which looks like half-digested almond cake mixed with tomatoes, and in the cabin my 'prosciutto e formaggio' bread-rolls take on a lurid, lysergic repulsiveness. My tummy is also oppressed by the distant explosion of plates beyond the cabin door. The plates are smashing like firecrackers as they slip on to the hard floor of the abandoned buffet. I force down some food and lay my head on the pillow – the very worst thing one could do. Within this tiny coffinlike retreat, all is rectilinear; all reference points are fixed; and yet the entire cabin is pitching about in the most drunken manner. This disjunction between the evidence of one's eyes (fixity) and the evidence of the other senses (lurcherama) produces swooning of the mind and nausea. Really it would be best to go back up on deck but I lack the resolve and am tossed biliously on the bunk, wondering why the hell I ever left my cosy flat in Notting Hill or the freezing flat in Palermo.

The reason for that–for the leaving–is simple. It's curiosity. Through the long, coal-black nights of an English winter, I have sat on the floor in front of the fire and pored over the atlas, imagining the world. The large sumptuous legends of escape–Gobi, Venice, Angkor–rarely set my imagination on a roll. They are overplayed. But certain small names have a miniature allure, as of a dream which is exotic but manageable, like a fantastic charm on the bracelet of life. Malacca, Noto, Swaziland, Cochin, Ootacamund, Akaroa, Galle, Diu, Petropolis, Eigg, Curaçao. Often there is a misfit quality to these places, crumbling backwaters whose day has gone, and if they manage to convey the impression that the clock stopped in 1929 I can get very excited: curiosity and the pursuit of novelty does not exclude the past. Far from it. Nostalgia is often the route to rebirth. That is what the word 'renaissance' means, rebirth, and the Renaissance in Europe was the rediscovery of the old classical world, a discovery which enabled Europe to escape from the suffocation of the Middle Ages into a healthier light. Nostalgia isn't a hankering for the past as such, but the desire to retrieve a loss. Sometimes it's purely the name, the very configuration of letters, which suggests the ideal, forgotten stopping place, especially if it contains a 'z' (Cadiz, Zanzibar) or an 'x' (Buxton, Xanadu). If they are positioned in warm climates they have to be visited out of the hot season because an endless battle with the sun severely curtails the psychic space which these resorts are intended to supply. And one mustn't catch some gruesome bug – that's not the idea at all.

In these respects Gozo appeared to have everything. An island off the north-east coast of Malta, it was integral to that British colony and occasionally visited by Governors from Valletta for recreation. Its capital Victoria was named in honour of the Queen on the occasion of her Diamond Jubilee in 1897, and in Victoria town there is listed only one hotel – the Duke of Edinburgh. Gozo's history is very old. Odysseus was shipwrecked there and entertained for seven years by Calypso, the nymph-daughter of Atlas. But there are remains of enigmatic temples built two thousand years before Homer. And it is said to be greener, sleepier, more seductive than its parent island of Malta. The inhabitants can speak plenty of English, make red wine, crochet lace, and drive on the left in the deep dark south of Europe within winking distance of Arabian Africa...

Meanwhile back in the cabin, I'm still going through it. The particular distress of sea-sickness is not only the sick feeling but the way it mimics certain forms of insanity. Confused perception, the arousal of subconscious fears, dissociation, and so forth. Vomit I do not however, and as suddenly as we fell into it, we are out of the plunging pull of water. Apparently the crossing is nearly always bad, this being the narrow and only sea-channel between the large bodies of the east and west Mediterranean; but to-day it has been made a great deal worse by the storms. Somehow the transition itself, to placidity, is unnoticed; there only comes a moment when it dawns on one that an agony has passed, that one is OK, that one is hungry. It is very difficult maintaining atheism at sea: I give thanks to

God in abject, tearful fashion and polish off the ham & cheese rolls.

With fearsome bangs on doors, the stewards pass down the corridor saying pack up, we'll be in port within the hour. And already night has fallen. Walking out on deck I face into a cold black wind and discern by degrees a fanlike glow in the distance like a sunrise in hell. This is the first hint of valiant Malta, a rocky riverless island which despite blockades and dreadful bombardments never surrendered to the Fascists in the Second World War. In 1942 King George VI awarded the entire citizenry the George Cross, which emblem has been incorporated into the national flag. Its population is reportedly of Carthaginian origin and the native language is of the Semitic family.

The approach and entry to the Grand Harbour of Valletta is a marvel I have not been prepared for. With the wind dropping and the water calming at every stage, bastion upon bastion of the greatest fortress in the world, tier upon tier climbing from knuckles of rock and floodlit a coppery orange, unfold their battlements and turrets in a slow, seemingly endless series of tableaux on either side of the channel. Above the wavy curtains of these massive walls, blue floodlight bathes classical buildings set among palm trees whose branches show up like tiny green herringbones. Sea-approaches are always magical – the finely graduated decoding of a mystery – and this approach to Valletta must be the most awe-inspiring in the Old World as that to Manhattan is in the New. Silently on smooth, jet-black water, the ship advances, saluted everywhere by this serrated magnificence.

Tucked on to a stone terrace is the Grand Harbour

Hotel, a far smaller affair than it sounds. A young man of immense girth attends the night desk and his trusting comportment is very noticeable after my period of living in Palermo tensions. He puts me in Room 67, tiny, with a view over luminous castled water. I sprawl on the bed, letting mental pictures sift themselves. Sleep comes slowly.

The following day it is warm, with a few detergent-white clouds in a flat blue sky, and I discover what that man on board must have meant by Sicily being 'civilisation': good food and stylish dress. Neither are Maltese attributes. But there is civilisation of another sort here: absolute safety in public places. I can walk where I want when I want. I can change money easily and quickly. The people are without suspicion or arrogance. None of that interminable Sicilian Arabo-Latin complication.

I also discover that the boat to Gozo leaves at lunch-time – soon! – and I scuttle aboard, slumping into a window seat with my luggage. The voyage isn't long and moves north-west along the Maltese coast, chugging past miles of ugly cement buildings. Oncoming – the bare creamy rock of little Comino Island – a relief – it is undefiled – and soon after, I scan the distant lineaments of Gozo...which isn't particularly green, and looks surprisingly built-up too, but the buildings at least are low. On the cliffs above Gozo's harbour several gothic-revival churches are brilliantly inappropriate.

Struggling ashore with bags, I am at once hailed from a car window by a taxi-driver. He reminds me of those trendy young men one sometimes met with in India who combined the cultures of several continents in a very odd way. This one has long hair drooping over his shoulders in black tendrils and he calls me 'mate', 'man' and 'sir' all in the same stream of chatter. I sling my large bag in the back with no help from him and sit beside it with the smaller one on my lap. The driver certainly knows the Duke of Edinburgh Hotel – but he's not impressed.

At a set of traffic lights on the harbour road we are obliged to stop and my attention diverts to a man standing in the street, one of more conventional appearance than the taxi-driver. This other man is about thirty years old, sturdily built with short curly hair, and he's on the kerb staring straight through the window at me. No doubt about it – I'm being 'clocked'. My skin prickles. His face has balanced features, but why its dark inquisitive eyes and somewhat irascible expression should be directed towards me I can't imagine. So at once on this island there is contact and a sense of, not hostility exactly but of, well, disquiet.

The Duke of Edinburgh Hotel is out of a novel by Lawrence Durrell or Malcolm Lowry. I am captivated the moment its Italianate façade appears at the bottom of Victoria's main street. The driver, pushing some of his tendrils behind one ear, tries to arrange future journeys with me but I tell him I'm going to rent a car, whereupon he says he has a friend who rents cars very cheaply and hands me a card with a phone number on it. As I pay the fare he adds 'There is an excellent Country & Western night at Marsalforn.' I notice he's wearing cowboy boots. I never see him or his like again.

The hotel foyer is shadowy and noiseless, spacious and cool, with old brown furniture which looks as though it's rooted to the floor. I expect someone to pop up from somewhere and ask me what I want but nobody does, so I slowly skirt the walls. To my amazement they are hung with type-written testimonials, now yellow with age, from the British Royal Family, the Governors of Malta, and Winston Churchill's private secretary, saying thank-you so much for this and for that, it was so very kind of you to do whatever and how wonderful your hotel is. Once upon a time, it would seem, this was quite a place but now the hotel is desolate – not a soul around – nobody – nothing. A few keys on hooks behind a dusty reception-desk of varnished wood are the only clue that we might be in a place of accommodation. As with the man at the traffic lights, its interest verges on the sinister.

Peering about, I edge my way into a murky vestibule and along a corridor lined with framed photographs. They too are from long ago, from the dance-band days before the war and a decade or so after it. The men wear black tie, the women sparkly evening-dresses; bottles chill in silver buckets on white damask tablecloths; and couples dance. Obviously the photographs were taken here, in the ballroom presumably, which looks art deco. Maybe it's through there…But I find myself in a bar, recently redecorated in the Gozitan Cotswold style – tapestry chairs and knobbly wooden tables – oh, a voice at my back has said 'Hullo'. It's not an unfriendly voice, and I do not jump, but turn round and reply 'Hullo'.

'Do you want to stay?' asks a dreamy young woman in jeans.

'I do please.'

'Only you?'

'Yes, that's right.'

Have I displeased her by being only me, or by wanting

to stay in the first place? It's impossible to work out what her curdled expression might mean. Maybe she's not displeased at all.

'Is anyone else staying here?' I venture.

'I think there's one couple staying...Some people moved out this morning...'

The bed & breakfast rate is of a cheapness which says that if you like you could stay here for ever, so at once I feel safe. She hands me Key Number 3, explaining that it's for Room Number 2, and calls mildly round the corner to an invisible presence which turns out to be an exceedingly tall chambermaid with a few long teeth in her upper jaw, who is persuaded to desert the mop-bucket and show me upstairs. The dreamy young woman smiles at last and melts away into a recess and I never see *her* again either.

The staircase displays more photographs, this time of the Royal Family itself, of both the official and unofficial kind, and they are hung so haphazardly as to suggest an irrepressible excitement: couldn't wait to get them up and don't care where they go. But now that the excitement has ebbed away, the photographs look random, poignant, even apprehensive.

At the top of the staircase I come to a large landing with a high ceiling. Its floor is laid with beautiful floral tiles, original nineteenth-century ones. A gilt mirror all foxed across, a console table and giant linen chest strive to an idea of grandeur whose appeal lies not in the achievement but in the attempt. After the shadowed uncertainty below it is so light-hearted up on this airy, flowery dancefloor of a landing, that I can't help letting out a little laugh or two. Big Bertha looks round at me and shuffles on again.

She really is one of the tallest women I've ever seen.

My room is a suite. Heavy double doors, once painted dark blue, open into an ante-room which has steps down to a bedroom with two beds, several cupboards, and another tiled floor in pretty colours. Beyond is a bathroom with ants scurrying round the bath-tub as though in a white rollerdrome. Overhanging it there's a water-heater which Bertha switches on with pride, flicking at the ants with a cloth. Her English is not superb and when I say I'm from London she grunts and says 'Yes, garden', opening a door of frosted glass on to a balcony above the rear of the hotel. There's a small swimming-pool out there containing no water. I divine at once that it will be possible to sit on the loo and stare through the open door at lemon and palm trees without being exposed. The balcony has a washing-line complete with wooden pegs and the afternoon sun streams on to it. Yes, one could live here for quite a while.

When Big Bertha has gone, half chuckling to herself, half amazed, having strenuously tried to refuse my tip, I test the bed. Comfy. Linen sheets, cream woollen English blankets, worn but spotlessly clean. Attached to the high ceiling is an electric fan which works. They tear out fans these days, lower the ceilings and install air-conditioning, but thankfully not here. I am describing the place in some detail because it is a rarity, an example of a kind of sanctum which has almost disappeared from the world. In how many tropical and subtropical rooms like this have I slugged from a bottle, or with luck kissed a neck smelling of sunshine, or opened a book, or daydreamed when the body has come to a horizontal halt but the mind is yet adrift with trains of thought flowing like silken scarves into empty spaces. The Fonseca Hotel, Aurangzeb Road, New Delhi, where I stayed with Sarah – it was a spacious Lutyens villa now demolished (someone said there is a Holiday Inn on the site). That fabulous hotel in Trivandrum with the teak interiors and white muslin mosquito-nets. It was called, I think, the Mascot. Is it still there and in proper shape? The Constellation in Vientiane, becalmed and mysterious during the monsoon season before the Communist take-over, or the Christina in Mexico City, with its vestigial French trimmings – do they retain anything of their anachronistic allure even if they are still extant? Those passé hotels with big cheap rooms, they were so sexy and useful, and heady with escape from personal history and with opportunity to live anew.

Victoria's main street, accelerating in steepness to the small central square with its red telephone box and red pillar box, is lined with classical buildings of high quality put up in the local golden stone. These include two enormous theatres, the Aurora and the Astra, each belonging to one of the island's two principal brass bands. At 9 pm it has grown cold and dark, the streets are empty, there is no passeggiata in this land, the Gozitans don't go out, and there isn't a single restaurant open, only a couple of bars lit by the heartless glare of strip lighting. Inside them a few gnarled peasants smoke and growl. From the citadel's breezy ramparts one sees perhaps as many as twenty churches presiding from as many hills, near and far, all picked out in yellow lightbulbs like Harrods or the Maharajah's palace at Mysore. It is a unique sight, so many large churches within such a small non-urban compass. They are lit like this because Easter is approaching, which for Christians is a mixture of misery and exultation, hideous death and weird resurrection, but which usually affects me more directly as the spring festival, joyous herald of the flowering year.

Back at the Duke of Edinburgh I discover the hotel restaurant is open, the only one in Victoria open at night-time, and I order a pizza which is all that's on the menu. Pizzas, seemingly, are what keep the hotel going. Mine is excellent, but the other diners don't give me so much as a glance and I retire to my room with the remains of a bottle of Gozitan red–good colour, robust taste, no tartness or trace of additives. It's called Bacchus Wine on its charming label–and so…here I am on the island with the wonderful four-letter name, with my muscles easing as the ruby liquid suffuses them. But now that I'm here–well, what am I going to do?

I think I am going to do nothing. It seems to be what the locals are doing. In which case I'd better rent that car. In places like this you require a car if you are to wander aimlessly, lest you find yourself having to take buses to specific destinations. The bedroom has grown chilly, so I switch on the heater. The only other guests in the hotel, the couple, are lodged in the suite next to mine, presumably for the maid's convenience. Through the wall the sounds of their love-making socialise the silence. No, I'm not envious. I have all that back in Palermo–otherwise, yes, I should be envious. And I don't grow a sympathetic erection either, but am rendered cosy by the pulsations from the other side of the wall as though we were three dogs in a kennel. Then I get an erection…

In the morning I awoke too early for breakfast, and

when I awoke again it was too late. In theory I always like to go down for breakfast–but in the event it's always a bind, falling out of the shower and into one's clothes and down the stairs in a mist of semi-wakefulness. Over at the car-hire, the agent pooh-poohs my enquiry of 'Do I leave a deposit?' This is remarkable, as is the fact that the car is one of half a dozen parked in the road outside his office, all of them unlocked with the keys inserted and ready to start. Surely we are in the only place in the entire Mediterranean region where such a thing is possible? The gears of mine are pretty much wrecked–it takes some fishing about to find one–but driving on Gozo is sheer honky-tonk pleasure. All roads splay out from Victoria, so basically you move in the direction you wish to go and trust to instinct. You may be on the wrong road but you cannot get lost.

Between stone-walled fields in a landscape of mesas and wild flowers, past yellow houses with green shutters, I head for the principal sight of the island, the prehistoric Ggantija Temples, but they are closed to-day and I judder on to Ramla Bay. I don't think it's warm enough to swim in the sea but you never know. Ramla is embraced by cliffs stacked in flakes and by terraces of maize and is overlooked by Calypso's cave. One of her caves, that is. Her various caves are disputed by historians. But this is the finest beach in a not very beachy archipelago and developers therefore are always trying to destroy it. The Government has resisted–to date. There are only three other cars parked where the road peters out. The sand is orange and blank except for a couple of stragglers, a van selling snacks, and a man with shaggy hair leading a donkey. An onshore wind has driven up the waves into frothing bands and I have a dutiful paddle where their extremities soak away into the sand. The water's freezing.

I forgot to bring a towel and so dry my feet with the socks before putting on plimsolls and unzipping a banana. Deep breaths. Lungs of ozone. This is the life. What next? Explore of course. On the far side of the beach are rocks beneath cliff paths and I am soon scrambling over them, steadying myself by grasping at bulges of stone. I'm doing quite well until, on looking down, I see that my plim-solls are smeared with tar. It's horrible. I'll probably have to throw them away. I examine the situation more closely. Enormous clots of the stuff cling to the bases of the rocks like a black death. Patches of what one believed to be a type of colour variation turn out to be this treacly filth. It's ghastly. It's criminal. It shouldn't be allowed. I'll have to climb to a higher track, one that is above the sea's deposit line along which tar has accumulated and which no doubt forms a satanic tourniquet extending round the whole island.

The higher track restores my equanimity a bit, because the views are panoramic, but before long this track too becomes impassable, waterlogged at vital points because of recent rain. Looking round for an alternative route, none is obviously available. But some distance ahead across the rocks I spy a figure, the first person I've seen since leaving the beach. He is walking towards me. So the way must be possible to negotiate somehow. Suddenly I realise that this is the man from the traffic lights, the one who gave me the fierce look through the taxi window. I hope he's in a better mood this time and I sit on a boulder to await his arrival. He will know all about the condition of the path.

But strange to say, he never does arrive. The track curves in and out of one's line of vision but the man does not again emerge into view. Where has he gone? I cannot see that it's possible for him to take another route–so has the earth swallowed him up? In a disturbing way I feel associated with his disappearance, in that had he not seen me, had I not been here, he would surely have passed by this boulder. In fact it's obvious that he's decided to avoid me. But how has he managed it? Is there a secret tunnel in the cliff? Or a grotto wherein he lurks, waiting to pounce on me should I proceed? Or is he crouching behind a rock until I've gone? I'll go back. Yes, that's what I'll do. I'll go back to the beach. Because for the first time in Gozo, or in Malta for that matter, I've experienced the warning bell of personal danger.

The wind has strengthened. I stumble around searching for shelter among the low dunes and scrubland...*that* looks like a choice spot over there, a sandy glade protected from the weather, and from onlookers, by thick bushes. But I pull up almost at once; it is already occupied. A middle-aged man is in there, reclining on a towel and reading a book. He doesn't resemble the frowning one in any way but wears a polo-neck sweater in a fine material of salmon-pink colour and his face is shaded by a straw hat with wide brim. I can see he has a white moustache clipped short but not much more. But on my sudden intrusion into his privacy he lays the book aside and looks up. 'Hullo,' he says. His eyes are very blue and seem pleased by the prospect of company, so we exchange smiles and introductions. His name is Gregory. He says he's a painter but it turns out that painting is only one of his activities. He seems more of a polymath as references to harpsichord music, Ancient Greek, geology, and much else, crop up in his conversation. 'I've been living on Gozo since 1968,' he says with neither relish nor distaste. It is far from his place of origin whose name I can't remember; it was somewhere in the USA.

'God, I bet you've seen some changes round here.'

'Oh, the centre of the island's almost filled up with houses. I think they're running out of stone. Do you know, I was reading an article on Postmodernism in architecture the other day, and the author said that Gozo is the only place where the production of the classical pillar has gone on uninterruptedly since the Roman Empire. Have you been swimming?'

'Are you serious?'

'Rain or shine, winter or summer, I swim every day,' he declares. 'But I don't sunbathe any longer. I had a touch of skin cancer which is now sorted out but that's why I'm done up like this.'

There is an outburst above us and both our heads turn. A shepherd boy, capering down the rocky hillside in S-shaped descents, is whooping and laughing as he leads his flock in a Gadarene run. The sheep dart hither and thither in unison like a school of fish. I look at Gregory, thinking he might say something, but he is now gazing sublimely out to sea through his translucent blue eyes, with the expression on his face of a stranded deity – thoroughly here, thoroughly not here, as if he has a great deal more space between his atoms than do most people. I pick up handfuls of sand and let the grains trickle slowly through my fingers.

After a few minutes he makes another observation. 'The atmosphere can sometimes be very unobstructive. Do you know, once or twice a year you can see Sicily from Ramla. And once in a decade you can see Aetna.'

'Do you go to Sicily much?'

'I don't go anywhere much. I have travelled. Widely. But now I stay here. I can hardly get it together to go into Victoria to have my eyes tested.'

'I met some Gozitans on the boat. They said that sailing up to Sicily was like sailing to civilisation. Did you find that?'

He thinks a while before replying: 'It probably depends on what you're looking for.'

In a place like Victoria, with nothing to do at night, with no radio or television or company in my room, I rediscover the fantastic power of cinema. I hunger for every film that comes on at the Aurora or Astra, any piece of trash. At the Aurora this evening I've seen *Diamond Skulls*, about extreme nastiness among the British upper classes. The Aurora's auditorium was built on a lavish scale in the nineteenth century, but gutted by fire, later refitted in the Festival of Britain style, and to-night there was a distinct pong of rotting fish weaving about inside. A mere two dozen customers partook of this giant space for the Saturday night show. And there was an interval. A proper one in the middle of the programme. Haven't known a proper interval at the cinema since the double-film shows of my boyhood or the two-part epic films of my adolescence. But they had one here. Of course it was a bit odd: they simply stopped the film mid-reel halfway through. Nobody did anything; no girl in a bonnet came round with ice creams on a tray slung from her neck; the film ground to a halt, the lights – red by the way – came up for ten minutes, went down again, and the film flickered back into life.

But this wasn't all that happened, because when the lights came up, bringing a break from the murderous mayhem on screen, I stood up to stretch my legs, looked round the great blood-red space, the mother of all wombs – and saw that man again, the traffic lights one, the man who'd vanished into the rocks. He was sitting about eight rows behind me and over to the left. I didn't like to stare because his dark features were lost in the umbra and I'd be unable to determine his eye. But it was the frowning one all right. I decided to walk out to the foyer as an excuse for a better glimpse of him, and as I passed he held his eyes rigidly ahead, deliberately not looking at me. Therefore – yes – he'd noticed me too. On coming back in, I didn't return to my former place but sat three rows behind him and observed how the red lamps reflected on his black curls. When the film restarted I was only tenuously reabsorbed by its unpleasant narrative. Quite a lot of the time I meditated on the back of the frowning one's head until – I don't know how it happened – it wasn't there any more. He'd gone. The man had gone. How could he have left without my noticing? He couldn't have done that. But he had. There was a quick flutter of panic. I felt ridiculous. I suppose I'd been more attentive to the film than I thought and he'd subtly slipped away. Who is he? And why is he playing these tricks on me?

Gozo is not fashionable. The last notables to live here were Nicholas Monsarrat who took to drink but who was writing up to a week before his death from cancer, and

Anthony Burgess who'd taken to drink long before arriving and 'who complained,' said Gregory, 'that Maltese Government censorship was so bad that he couldn't receive some of his own books!' The reason for its unfashionableness is the food, which if anything is even worse than on Malta, which means it's the worst food I've ever encountered, worse even than Poland's (my visit to Russia lay in the future). They simply have no awareness of nutrition or taste at all, and the food shops are filled with rock-hard rubbish and are often dirty. But there's a small supermarket selling British and German tins and sadly (on those days when I can't face another hotel pizza or afford the only decent restaurant, Salvina's) I'm relying on these plus vitamin pills. The menu attached to the snack-van at Ramla Bay reads: spaghetti & chips, hot dog, hamburger, fried egg, white bread & butter. When one lunchtime I went to its counter, the only things I could bring myself to buy were a bottle of soda water and a packet of banana chewing-gum manufactured in South Korea.

To-night (to-day being the Feast of Our Lady of Sorrows) a Madonna is paraded through the central square, supported by grim or giggling males, and accompanied by rocking candles in red glasses. The effigy is followed at snail's pace by a baby Austin van inside which a big peasant priest, his knees forced up under his chin, drones intonements through a crackly loudspeaker strapped to the roof. Around it, and behind, shuffles a throng of Gozitans in subfusc clothes, muttering responses. Some German tourists, jazzily attired, are silenced by the spectacle, and look on motionlessly until one of them takes a photograph, and the spell is broken, and they disappear noisily down the hill.

Overhead meanwhile, thousands of birds are screaming in the trees. Their multiple, overlapping chirrups grate violently on the eardrums. The triple conjunction – shuffling Gozitans, jazzy Germans, screaming birds – makes me feel sick. Why this particular form of helplessness should strike, I don't know, but I'm not surprised by it and decide to return to the refuge of my room and an evening with a book, a bottle of Bacchus, and tins.

A Sicilian friend of mine has a theory that the people of the sea are more intelligent than the people of the mountains because sea-air confers some chemical advantage to the development of the brain. The Gozitans seem not to support his theory in that, though generally good-natured when you do get through to them, they are not conversationalists or mentally agile. Rationality isn't their strong suit either. So to-night in the bar of my hotel it takes persistence to extract from the owner's son that the hotel is over one hundred years old and has always had the same name. For some reason he feels this is compatible with its being named after the Duke of Edinburgh who is the husband of Queen Elizabeth II. Such elementary failure of logic is what can stun you hereabouts and, as so often, one wonders whether religion be the cause or effect of such a condition. In fact the hotel must be named after the previous holder of the Edinburgh title, Prince Alfred, 'Affie', Queen Victoria's fourth child, who married the daughter of Tsar Alexander II. (Subsequent research discloses that Affie was also Commander of the Mediterranean Fleet, a keen violinist, and a collector of stamps which on his death in 1900 he left to the British Museum.)

The hotel is very conveniently situated. All the amenities of the town – bank, post office, newspaper shop, the Rundle Gardens, the two theatres, the Telemalta overseas telephone service – are only a few steps from its front door. I must tell you – I was phoning from the Telemalta office yesterday and asked for a London directory. They didn't have one; they had very few directories. 'We have this,' said the pretty girl, eager to help, and she handed me the directory for Costa Rica.

Good Friday. The Crucifixion of Our Lord. Why do they call it 'good'? It's like Sunday with knobs on, a gloom of the spirits so palpable you could bottle it and sell it as paperweights. Every flag is at half-mast. The theatres have placed crosses over their entrances and from the balcony of the Aurora two loudspeakers broadcast tapes of their brass-band blowing sedate Victorian and Italian marches and slow dance tunes, all in minor keys, with very miserable effect. The failure to hit notes adds an extra blighted touch and all is smeared into a whine by the poor quality of the sound system. A little boy and girl holding hands stare up perplexedly at the speakers as though trying to work out how the awful noise got up there.

Gozo's relative treelessness means that the salt air carries right across the island and when it isn't hot this makes the air clammy and chill. There is consequently a stickiness to the bedcover over which I am this afternoon extending my limbs, with a bunch of pillows at the head, reading Pope's *The Rape of the Lock* while, between verses, I fitfully consider my solitary state...There is nothing to worry about. Which can sometimes induce a free-fall vertigo because worries are the banisters of life. But at present, no free fall. Thoughts and impressions pass through me in leisurely, comprehensible chains of reflection. Yet the very blankness of the worry sheet supplies a surface on which a fine seismic needle can now and again scratch a distant unease and it takes mere moments to realise that this unease derives from the frowning one. In a busier world I'd not notice it – or him – but here…well, I suppose without unease there can be no adventure. Unease is the awareness of exposure, of possibility, that something else might happen. Unease brings alertness – which means that Gozo is not bland. The couple next door appear to have left. I am now the hotel's only guest. I wonder if I shall be the only person in the building when they close up at night. I do hope not. From the balcony the garden looks dull and damp. I come back in and give the book on the bed a shove with my knee. A shudder passes between my shoulderblades. I look round, and again I look round. My pulse quickens. Suddenly I am anxious.

The island still has a touch of what the Mediterranean had before tourism hit it, a self-sufficient character which is intimately connected to its drawbacks. Don't moan so much about the food. Good food demands a more aggressive culture. And if British rule must take some responsibility for the dreadfulness of the food, it can also take some for the probity of the population, both features being untypical of the southern world. Gozo will do you no violence. Even the dogs are gentler than Sicilian dogs. And I haven't seen a single beggar here, nor on Malta, not a single one. As I'm reminding myself of all this, a church bell begins to toll, not a carillon jangle but a bell single and sweet, and I feel the fear seep out of me. With every successive clang I am calmed. Surely the point of religion is to present existence in a positive light and to keep evil spirits in check. But religion doesn't do that. It emphasises our failings, our sins, our worthlessness, the ghastly destiny which awaits those who do not obey. Heaven becomes absurdly remote, nirvana an impossibility except via tortuous paths. Nearly all theology is a form of nightmare. But a few sweet things do sometimes come through. The lighting of a candle for example. Or the beauty of a quiet old building when the inane squeal of theology is stoppered. Or the sound of this single bell. It is now 10.45 pm and stepping on to the balcony I see a cross of golden lightbulbs on top of a church, greeting me over the roofs of the town, including me, embosoming me, piercing the circumference of the self so that any lingering fretfulness leaks away and I flow in a larger, more benign rhythm. This I believe is what is meant by communion. I fire up the water-heater and run a scalding bath. On this night I sleep very well.

Thus far the rain has held off but the Easter weather is not good. On Saturday powerful gales drive across the island from the direction of Greece and the sky is skidding lead. At Ramla Bay, shielded by shrubbery, Gregory says 'I'm sorry about the weather' in his carefully modulated Harvard voice, as though the climate were his personal responsibility.

'It's OK. It makes it like Cornwall,' I say. 'Will you swim?'

'This very second.'

He peels off his knitted salmon skin and totters down the sand into a heavy sea, a fragile but somehow protected figure. One does not fear for him. Periodically his head becomes visible; occasionally a flailing arm. Five minutes later he's staggering back up the beach, murmuring 'Oh God...oh God...'

'Isn't it dangerous?'

'Yes. This sort of weather can generate a terrific current in the bay like a fast-flowing river. But I know where to go, along by those rocks.'

'Those mucky rocks. I was reading *The Rape of the Lock* and –'

'I love that bit at the end,' he says, 'about the birth of a comet. *The heavens bespangling with dishevelled light...*'

His quotation so charms me that I forget what I was myself going to say about the poem, and mention instead that 'I thought I'd drive over to Marsalforn and check it out. Would you like to come?'

'That's kind of you. But I'm waiting for someone. In fact he may not turn up, but I'll wait anyway, in case he does.'

Over at Marsalforn, Gozo's main and shabby tourist resort, the sea is in magnificent uproar. Waves crash across the promenade and girls shriek with delight at the rocketing douches. Young bloods cruise slowly in dilapidated fuckmobiles and a large party of London schoolchildren, wearing dayglo clothes and with sharp haircuts, gossip furiously in a café – their animation marking them out as not local.

At teatime the rain arrives, sluicing the island without pause. Back at the hotel a mothers' meeting is going on in the Cotswold bar among a caterwaul of babies. Big Bertha waves to me from the dining-room. She is doing her best to be a waitress but 'grace under pressure' is not a characteristic of hers. On her way to the kitchen she asks

'How is Princess Diana?'

'Very well thank-you.'

'But they say she is sad in the newspaper.'

'Yes, I think she is.'

'You know her?'

'No, I don't know her.'

'But you have met her?' she asks, with a forward, beseeching movement of her shoulders, as though to be with one who's been with the Princess Diana would bestow a rosy light.

'I'm afraid not. But she once sat behind us at a Tina Turner concert.'

'We love Diana.'

Ah, yes, the Princess—it is remarkable how so many people whom Diana has never met, and does not know, have intimate and rewarding relations with her. I think even her enemies in England find themselves helplessly excited and gilded by the fact that the most glamorous woman on the planet is English and that in consequence our whole society there is lifted up a little more by the world's attention. I'd been with my friend Von at that Tina Turner concert—one of Tina Turner's numerous 'farewell' concerts—it was at Woburn Abbey—and Princess Diana is probably the only woman alive who could have upstaged Tina. But she did it in the most bashful way, arriving unaccompanied except for bodyguards, giving a self-deprecating little wave when she was picked out by a spotlight as she took her seat, to a huge cheer of appreciation from the audience. One of the detectives sat on Von's left, and turning to him she said 'Di's the first royal to show her knees' (the detective replied 'Is that so, love?').

The hotel owner's son is also in the bar, babyfying, and I tell him how I've fallen in love with his hotel.

'Oh good,' he replies, 'and it will be even better soon.'

'What do you mean, better?'

'We will develop.'

I go cold. 'Develop?'

'The bank won't lend us money for improvement unless we become a four-star hotel and the Government won't give us four stars unless we do the improvement – so to get the loan we must demolish the hotel.'

I feel slapped. He must have noticed this in my expression because he adds 'Oh, don't worry, we'll keep the façade on the street. We'll certainly keep the façade.'

'But the place is as solid as a rock. It doesn't need demolition. That's a complete waste of money.'

'You should write and tell our bank manager.'

'So what about the high ceilings and fans and the flowery, tiled floors?'

'Bulldozer.'

'It's mad.'

'That's what my father says.'

'And Big Bertha?'

'Who?'

'Can I have a whisky?'

Certainly there is case for doing the place up. It's not making the best use of itself. But really the nineteenth-century front half and the nineteen-twenties back half need only a clever, caring hand to turn this into a smart operation. That's probably what's missing. The cleverness.

'So after the summer,' he says, 'the bulldozers arrive. September 1st.'

I clutch at a straw. 'Why not demolish the nineteen-twenties bit at the back and keep the rest?'

'No. Demolish all.'

That's right. All. And they won't retain the street façade. Of course they won't. Too much trouble. They'll get rid of the lot and stick up a box. I reach my room in despair, wade through a packet of dates, and pop a vitamin pill, while the rain pours down the window. This is the only hotel on Gozo with any history or personality. Therefore it has to be demolished. Haven't they heard, in this wretched ditch of blinkered bank managers, that these days you restore? Sense of place is *in*, mate! The fading royal photographs, the imperial plaudits from the Palace at Valletta, the spacious period charm, everything will be swept away. Already I am mourning the hotel's death, seeing clearly that the room wherein I lie will be two rooms, maybe four, a new floor slicing horizontally through my ribcage, an air-conditioned blast stinging the nostrils, polyester sheets bringing on prickly heat.

I pour a big glass of Bacchus, not a good idea on top of whisky. Suddenly the ghosts of the place are very strong, aroused by imminent obliteration – scraps of chat about garden parties and illicit sex, threaded by echoes of foxtrot music – yes, the English this way came, bearing cocktails and epaulettes – you can hear them laughing and sighing, drinking, ruling, playing gramophone records and tennis, being languidly noble and controlling continents with a sardonic remark or a casual gesture born of romance and rectitude and boredom and fun, their blue eyes looking across a blue sea to beyond the horizon – nostalgia hisses into the room like a gas, as asphyxiating as a faceful of

Pre-Raphaelite arum lilies. Nostalgia, loss, melancholy, are these not forms of love?

Actually I feel awful. More Bacchus wine please. Yes, such a charming label. I must take a few bottles away with me. Because I shall leave Gozo now. Can't live here for ever, after all. The clock which stopped is moving once more. Time starts eating again, with a crunchy noise like that of the deathwatch beetle.

Easter Sunday. I drive to Ramla to say good-bye to Gregory – he is, as always, there. And so, to my great surprise and fascination, is – the frowning one. In a small place such as Gozo I must have seen a number of strangers several times over, but because they have not attracted my attention these recurrences pass unnoticed, fail to be granted the accolade of 'synchronicity'. Not the frowning one however. Him I notice every time. And to-day he is not frowning but playing on the sand with two toddlers, obviously his own, while a young woman, obviously his wife, looks placidly on. The weather is better than yesterday's and quite warm and the sun is out. Even so, he's the only man on the beach who's taken his top off. Once in a while he stands hands on hips, looking round, displaying the T-shape of hair on his muscled chest. The four of them potter for a further fifteen minutes or so, the man readopts his shirt, and they clamber into an old jalopy and drive off.

'I'm leaving to-morrow.'

'Ah...Come back again one day,' says Gregory.

'Yes, I shall. Perhaps I shall.'

For an Easter holiday the beach is surprisingly deserted. A couple walking dogs, three schoolboys sitting on scooters near the snack-van. We talk about the food situation, our experiences taking LSD, odds and ends. It's very restful.

'They are going to pull down the Duke of Edinburgh Hotel,' I say.

'Are they?' Gregory responds vaguely. 'That's a shame. I haven't been there for years. Here, let me give you this.'

He pulls a bag from under a bush and forages in it and produces a small painting done on a square of hardboard. It is vaguely Islamic in manner, with some kind of gold lettering appearing out of a cosmic whoosh, but subtle.

'Oh, Gregory, that's so kind. What do the letters say?'

'Don't worry about that. It's my own language. Look – the sun's come out.'

'Your own language?'

'Yes. I invented a language. And an alphabet to go with it.'

'Gregory, excuse me for a moment.'

I break away, churlishly in the circumstances. But it's because I've spotted – guess who. He's in the distance but I recognise the frowning one immediately. He must have dropped the family at home and come out again, for he's by himself, walking with determined stride round the rocky headland where I spied him once before. As I jog across the beach he turns a corner out of my sight but I keep following, climbing energetically beyond the tar line. I'm excited. The Spanish poet Cernuda refers somewhere to being 'sweetly confused, like a man anticipating some pleasure,' and Eric Rohmer in one of his films mentions the torments of anticipation. It's something like that, but more – I am in pursuit.

The route grows more awkward, the rocks more extravagantly shaped. I'm slowed right down and find myself scrambling through what resembles a lunar land-scape of mini-ravines and crags. I've never been this far round. Tumbled boulders form small enclosed spaces. Here and there, the stone has been worn flat by the diluvial lick – hidden sunbathing nooks in the season but now as silent as the grave.

Pausing to catch my breath, I scan for indications. Per-haps he knew a shortcut to wherever he's going, a secret passage through the maze of rocks. The terrain slopes sharply up from the shore and it looks as though in a couple of places there has been recent landslip...Then I register – not a noise exactly – perhaps a signal slightly beyond the range of the conscious senses – anyway a piece of information which causes me to climb carefully and peer between rocks.

Not far away, in a sheltered scoop, I see him. His clothes have been removed and lie in a jumbled heap. He is naked, his shaggy haunches moving slowly against someone, who is also naked. The golden expanse of his back prevents dis-closure of who the other is and anyway they are kissing softly, face to face. He stops, twists his torso, turns his head and sees me...

Blood rushes up through my whole body, tingling hotly into head and face. He turns further. There is a flash of white teeth – he's grinning! His erect penis bobs in the sunshine. He makes a gesture to me with his left arm and turns back to his partner, a young male. The gesture was entirely ambiguous. It could have meant either go away, you intruder, or come, join us in pleasure. When I was a little boy, if some uncertainty was frightening – if I thought I saw a ghost or someone's behaviour confounded me – my whole instinct was to run towards the uncertainty in order to resolve it and dispel it. In growing up I've acquired skills and knowledge and experience, but at heart how much more am I than that little boy? Perhaps I am less in resilience and courage. But of course little boys aren't consciously sexual. Sexual awakening brings doubt, and with doubt the hiatus of hesitation and the possibility of misunderstanding. Little boys are active; they don't understand. For several moments, my heart thumping painfully, I am spellbound by the secret lovers. But it is too much, I must escape this quandary, and instead of going towards them, I scurry quickly away over the rocks like a frightened crab... By the time the sand is reached, my body and mind have become amazingly focused and my whole being overtaken by the profoundest dissatisfaction. And Gregory has packed up and gone home.

Back at the hotel Big Bertha is cleaning my apartment – at 5 pm. Apologetically I take off my tarry shoes and find a newspaper to set them on. She says 'To-morrow good sun'. I say 'To-morrow I leave' and give her some money before she escapes. Again she tries to refuse it, as though suspicious of what it's for.

Lying on the bed, my eyelids gently close – and snap open again. What was that about nostalgia and melancholy being forms of love? They are forms of paralysis! The sense of loss – enough of it! Let the pull of the past be succeeded by the pull of the future and the sense of loss replaced by the sense of expectancy. Our world is embodied contradiction, our lives possible only in the fluctuations of reciprocity, and now it is the turn of the future. Besides, I've run out of books and there is not a proper bookshop on the island. If I stay I shall be forced, like Gregory, to invent my own language, and a private language is one paradox I don't go for. Hot water gushes into the bathtub and shampoo makes fragrant foam. To-morrow – another boat, another destination.

CHAPTER TWO

The Curious Case of Bapsy Pavry

OOTACAMUND 1975 — There wasn't a cloud in the sky and Rita Wallace, Sarah Moffett and myself were steaming up the side of the Nilgiri Hills in a little blue train. The wheels moved so slowly that sometimes we seemed to be hanging motionless among green coffee plantations, hardly breaking the cool air. 'Nilgiri' means 'blue' and by the time we arrived it was evening and blue mists were threading the valleys. First appearances however were a shock. We'd been told that Ooty, Queen of the Hill Stations, possessed houses like those of Sunningdale in the English stockbroker-belt, and that its setting had the airy drama of Northumberland, and that it was the last word in subcontinental gentility. To underline this expectation I had in Delhi come across a book of sepia postcards from its heyday circa 1920 in which Ooty looked immaculate. Yet here we were in some derelict station with a lot of mess going on down by the railway tracks. Rita was a divorcée and a redhead. She looked up at me. Her face in recent days had been blistered by the sun and there was entreaty, even despair, in it. I tried to be encouraging and said 'I hear there are lieutenants at Wellington down the road.' Her smile was touched with sadness. It was more than fatigue.

A skinny porter in oily turban grabbed our bags, high-stepped across shiny railway lines, and deposited them at a trackside hotel. The matter was literally taken out of our hands but after three days of travelling – we'd left Kovalam on the morning of St Valentine's Day by bumpy bus for Quilon, grateful for the pellets of opium we'd stirred into hot coffee, and took the inland boat at nightfall from Aleppey to Cochin and after that a sleepless but dreamy train journey via Coimbatore to Mettupalayam – and after all that, we had acquired the open-ended fatalism in the eternal present which is said to characterise non-European temperaments, and so had followed the porter submissively.

The large room in which we found ourselves contained half a dozen single beds. It would do for a night. Supper consisted of omelettes with bread, butter and tea at a table in the hallway, and we ate gratefully but without talking. Don't know what the time would have been. But in our dormitory, slumped across the beds, which were all out of alignment and arranged in no purposeful manner, we smoked grass, finished off the Indian whisky, and crashed out. In those days marijuana was easily available everywhere for a nod and a wink and a few rupees, and usually came in twiggy clumps wrapped in newspaper, much like fish & chips in the United Kingdom.

In the middle of the night Rita woke me with a scream. She said something had touched her. I said she'd imagined it and we went back to sleep. Some time later she screamed again and said she wasn't imagining it and she could hear something as well – couldn't I hear something, a scraping noise, a crunching noise? Our attention was riveted to the black silence.

'I can hear Sarah snoring,' I said at last.

Next, with an awful yell, Rita propelled herself across the room and into my bed. 'I've been bitten, you sod!'

Dutifully I slid out of bed, and went across to the door, and fumbled around on the wall for the light-switch. Before I'd found it, something with claws ran over my bare instep. I froze. Moving the switch frantically up and down and sideways, I managed to get the striplight to flicker into cold life and shot back to bed too. From above the parapet of our blanket, we looked and saw nothing, nothing at all, and so cautiously I crept across the room again and flung Rita's mattress into the air and on to the floor. Holes had been ripped in its underside and tufts of flock stuck out. I lit a cigarette, watched and waited. Before long a black snout, followed by a pair of sharp black eyes, pushed outwards from a hole in the floor near the door and after twitching about a bit the eyes were followed at a squeeze by a plump body. Soon four rats were slithering over the mattress, pulling at the stuff and eating it with prayerlike movements of their paws.

'Why aren't they afraid of the light?' wondered Rita.

I threw my unfinished cigarette at them. They didn't flinch. I lit matches from a box and threw them too. Our accommodation these past weeks had run the gamut from beach-shack to palace, and there would be rats again, but never a group so bold as these on our first night in Ooty. They weren't hostile but were utterly indifferent to us and their indifference and self-possession were mesmerising. Rita fell asleep again, pushing an assortment of protruberances into my back. In many ways she was much more adaptable than I. It took me three more cigarettes before I could even think of settling down. Sarah had been sleeping loglike throughout, presumably on the Mandrax substitutes we'd found in a Trivandrum chemist.

Sarah Moffett had an American father and an English mother and I was her flatmate in London. We were doing our own wonky version of the hippy trail, following on from some crazy experiences at the first ever Delhi Film Festival. When we turned up at the Ashoka Hotel in Delhi the organisers were kindness itself. They gave Sarah full accreditation as my secretary for the whole fortnight, along with all the perks and allowances which that entailed. Couldn't have been sweeter, and I must attempt to write about it one day because it turned into the most outrageous freebie of our lives. Afterwards the arts editor at the *Spectator*, Kenneth Hurren, said 'But aren't you coming back to attend to your career?', a view put to me more forcefully by my father six months later. But I thought that's what I was doing. I've always been free-lance. And they knew it was my intention to move on through the East and that my return air-ticket to London was open for a year. Rita Wallace was also a close friend—I'd met her through the transsexual pioneer April Ashley (they'd been bohemians together in Paris in the 1950s); Rita had been staying with the de Mel family in Colombo and flown to Trivandrum aerodrome to join Sarah and myself for a little adventure.

The local coffee and an argument with the patron, to whom we consented to pay only half the bill on account of the rats, proved bracing, as did the Nilgiris themselves. The more you strayed from the railway station and what was called 'the native village', the nicer Ooty became. The centre of town is called Charing Cross and from here a policeman on a dais directed what little traffic there was. Beyond it, the purlieus fanned up and about in leafy lanes. Clambering thither in our search for somewhere attractive to stay, somewhere perhaps Sunningdalian, we chanced upon the Emerald Heights Ladies College. They spoke of the poet Browning and said they didn't let rooms and gave us Marmite sandwiches and mugs of tea at a long refectory table which seemed to disappear into the distance.

One of the schoolmistresses recommended the Officers' Holiday Home and pointed her finger in its direction. So along one of the lanes in late afternoon we dragged our weary feet and in due course came to a low shingled villa. It spread itself comfortably behind flower-flecked hedges and pine trees and there was a little lodge at the entrance to the drive. Its full name, on a polished brass plate beside the front door, was the Ratan Tata Officers' Holiday Home. It looked divine.

The establishment was under the guardianship of an ex-Indian Army officer who told us to call him Inkie because everybody else did. The charm of the place became even greater when we discovered that Inkie was actively concerned for our welfare, especially for Rita's rat-bite which had swollen up nastily on her calf. Inkie assured us there were no rats in his domain, and having negotiated a rate – the equivalent in rupees of £1.50 per head per day full board – we joined a handful of inmates for a fortnight's rest, and washed and changed for dinner.

That night Rita wore cream muslin, Sarah a floor-length wraparound skirt and plunging granny-top, and I yellow flared trousers and a tight black Spanish jacket with bobbles round the edge. The black jacket had been presented to me on departure by another of our flatmates in London, Frances Shelley. She said it had been a godsend when she was in India, had got her everywhere, and as you know hippy clothing was very trans-gender. It got me everywhere too and the black bobble jacket became my standard evening dress on this travelling-light journey through India and the East. Travelling light, yes, but I was away for ages, and it's amazing how you can cram a whole life into a bag when you're young. It helped that I was skinny. In fact Inkie thought I needed feeding up and said 'Here you will have an appetite. We are seven and a half thousand feet above sea level.' Well, I'd not lost my appetite as such, but French 'blues' – the soft uppers manufactured by Smith, Kline & French which Sarah and I bought in local chemists and always had a supply of – have a tendency to render one unhungry (or did – they don't make them any more). We also had the 'yellows' – Dexedrine – unadulterated uppers; whereas the 'blues' combined Dexedrine with a dash of downer, so had their contemplative side.

In the dining-room the tallest of the gardeners had also changed, into a red and green jacket many of whose brass buttons had dropped off or almost had. He served us Brown Windsor soup, lamb and three veg, and junket which was scalded on top with cinnamon and nutmeg. The pudding was particularly good, and when we told the gardener so, he said the cook would make us the same again right away.

A famous ornithologist called Major Kashir was on leave and at the next table, trying to slap some table manners into his elder son, a morose boy. The younger son was milder, making no sort of challenge but taking it all in no doubt for the day when his pubic hair sprouted and he'd answer back. The Major's wife leant across to us and asked 'Are you having a lovely time?'

'Oh we are,' beamed Rita, 'apart from my rat-bite.' Mrs Kashir looked horrified, so Rita quickly added 'Not here! Near the station.'

Mrs Kashir wanted a change of subject nonetheless, and she was also a little embarrassed by the atmosphere between her husband and her sons, so she said to us 'Come outside a moment. I should like to show you something.'

Since it was more of an instruction than a request, we stood up and walked past our waiter who halted against a background of fake-brick wallpaper, the second junket on his hands. The Major remained seated, brushing potato out of his moustache with a napkin, while the sullen sons were commanded not to move an inch. 'Not an inch!'

Outside in the garden, Mrs Kashir pointed into the navy-blue night above the conifers and asked 'Do you see that?'

'No.'

'That. Look. There. Above the fourth tree from the left. A star.'

'Oh, yes. I see.'

'So it's a star,' said Miss Moffett.

'My dear–wrong. It's not a star. I've been watching it for several days. It's getting closer.'

Rita shivered inside her shawl–it was February–and asked 'How much closer?'

Mrs Kashir shrugged. 'Who knows? Maybe it will crash into us.'

'But how do you know it's getting closer?' asked Sarah.

Mrs Kashir pounced. She wanted to mystify us. 'On Thursday it was over there! Above the eighth tree!' And retied her headscarf and buttoned up the fawn car-coat which she always wore over her beautiful saris. 'It's definitely not a satellite, one may say, because it takes a zig-zag course, some nights higher, some nights lower. To-night it's higher. And the reason I know it's getting closer is–every night brighter! If you eye it askance, you will see that it is a greenish colour. Can you see that?'

We couldn't.

'Well, I've been observing it longer than you. It is undoubtedly a mechanical object.'

Rita told Mrs Kashir that her car-coat looked very warm and the lady answered 'Oh, it is. Terywool, you know.'

We passed a green baize noticeboard in the hall. Sarah nosed among the pinned-up messages and discovered that a jumble sale was happening a few days hence in aid of the roof of St Stephen's Church, and we decided to go along since it was nearby. Inkie told us that Ooty's founder, John Sullivan, is buried in St Stephen's whose arches were taken from the palace of Tipoo Sultan. Also within walking distance, according to the town map, were the Nilgiri Library, the Ootacamund Club, and Spencer's Grocery Store where they sold Dundee Cake, Oxford Marmalade and Cheddar cheese; while to reach the Assembly Rooms, where English and American films were occasionally shown, you had only to follow gravity down a number of stepped paths.

The next morning (amphetamine-orange pee in a bright yellow loo) I felt in need of intellectual stimulus. Rita and Sarah invaded the Junk Emporium in a gothic-revival stableyard opposite the Ratan Tata while I took off for the Nilgiri Library which is a famous institution. It was founded in 1859 and the building resembles a red Victorian vicarage, with a reading room like a school-hall jutting into the rear garden. Inside, the walls were adorned with stuffed tiger and stag heads. Novels, popular biographies and children's books were downstairs while the more valuable part of the collection was upstairs where the Warden, Mr Lincoln Townsend, had his office. He was middle-aged and his manner combined Oxford don with Chief Scout, and it turned out that his family came from Leicestershire. Most impressive was the office itself whose proportions were archiepiscopal. Nobody could sit in quarters like that and be a wimp.

'I'll take you for a drive in my jeep if you like,' he offered at our first meeting.

'That's very kind, Mr Townsend.'

'Lin, call me Lin, like the Chinese laundry.'

It must have been a colonial-type joke. I noticed he cracked it whenever he met someone new, and I still don't get it.

'Do you want to look downstairs first? You'll find Roy Kugler there. He's a fool, so I gave him the novels to sort out where he could do no harm.'

At first Roy Kugler, thin and bony, was in amiable spirits, reminiscing about his Burmese trading days in a distinct Derbyshire accent. But a great gust of irritation suddenly overwhelmed him and he declared 'To be honest, I have no patience with this sort of thing!' – meaning my visit to the Library – but I was the only person there! – and he stormed off.

Blinking, I go back upstairs and ask if I've done anything wrong. Lin says 'Don't mind him. I told you he was a fool.'

'Don't you ever feel like going back to England?'

'I did go back once a few years ago when my father died. But I couldn't live there any more, it's been too long. It would be like being shut inside a kitchen garden. How should I exist? A tiny house on the south coast? I'd die! I still think of the UK as home but only at a distance.'

He was speaking inside a colossal Victorian fireplace with ornamental overhangs from which he emerged like a majestic troglodyte when his manservant Monica (yes, that's right) entered the room with a tray of coffee. Monica stepped across piles of books to reach Lin's teak desk laden with ledgers and inkpots. When later I came to spend time working in this library, Monica would bring me a pot of coffee for one rupee a go.

Lin, staring over his half-moon spectacles, asked 'Do you take sugar?'

'Not usually. But to-day I shall.'

'Do you like India?'

'Yes.'

'What do you like about it?'

'Like isn't the word actually. Sometimes it's very hard work. But it doesn't feel alien. This library for example reminds me of my school. And one is never asked to explain one's presence. It's as though one were expected.'

'Being an expatriate makes me realise that all life is temporary,' he replied.

'Can I look round up here?'

'Do – do…'

Copies of *The Yellow Book* were wedged against Marie Corelli's thirty-seven-page rodomontade on Victoria, *The Greatest Queen in the World* (Skeffington's of Piccadilly, 1900 – I read it during a violet, green and tangerine sunset); *The Illustrated Sporting and Dramatic*, the *Westminster*, *Edinburgh*, and *Contemporary* reviews; *Baily's*, *Fraser's*, *Blackwood's*; shelf upon shelf of royally bound obsolescence; and one morning a Scarlet Minivet chirruped in a cedar outside the window as I flicked through

Louise Jordan Miln's *When We Were Strolling Players in the East*. The character of the upstairs collection is that of the British Empire weekending and this is probably the last conservatory for it outside museums. I became particularly entranced by an old guidebook, *Ooty and Her Sisters, or Our Hill Stations in South India*, published by Higginbothams of Madras in 1881, authored by 'Geofry' (yes, spelt that way) whom Lin identified as Geofry Ryan, an English coffee-planter of those times. 'Effect of Mountain Air on European visitors...To see him skipping like a deer over the heights you might fancy he had got invisible balloons under his armpits.' Geofry wants to get rid of the native village: 'Surely the knocking down of this small village and building a better where it could never contaminate the lake, is as nothing when we look at Peter the Great and his great city! Is not our righteous government greater than he?' Well, the native village is still there, gradually taking over and driving the European elements into ever lonelier corners.

Back at the Ratan Tata there was a perceptible tightness between the two women. Rita was small and round with a beautiful face. She was the first woman I ever slept with (she took charge; I was hopeless), and was one of the most cheerful people you could meet. To use a cliché: she lit up a room when she entered it–even if you didn't want it lit up. Her vivacity had survived serious rebuffs, including a failed marriage. One of the first things she told me, when she came to my rooms at Folly Bridge in Oxford, was that while pregnant with their last child, her husband had spat in her face and she could always feel the spittle running down her cheek whenever she thought of it.

Concerning that strange relationship with her American husband, who was an academic, who obviously loved her at first, it was the only self-pitying thing she ever said. He was disinherited by his father as a result of the divorce. Rita's father-in-law, a very rich man who'd been involved with the development of sonar navigation or something of the sort, asked her not to make a scandal for the family by demanding her dues and in return he'd make generous provision for her privately. Rita, who couldn't bear the idea of court proceedings, readily agreed; but almost immediately afterwards her father-in-law went into a coma from which he never emerged and Rita and her children got no settlement at all. Funnily enough I think Sarah's father had been disinherited by his father for the same reason, divorce.

Even at seven and a half thousand feet, the Indian climate doesn't suit redheads, and neither do rats, and Rita had grown muted. But something else had happened. Had the women had some kind of squabble? There was a froideur between them. Sarah was in the more confident position psychologically, having been on the road with me for months. She was looking fit and tanned. Her long floating hair was streaked with sunshine, as was mine. Also she was younger than I, Rita older, and such things are more important to women than to men, or anyway more important to the women on this occasion than to me. When I came in from my library visit Sarah perked up diplomatically and said 'Look what I bought at the junk shop,' and plonked on her head a flowered nineteen-thirties hat. Its label read 'Modern Modes, The Pantiles, Tunbridge Wells'. Rita, who'd been looking out of the window, turned round and exclaimed 'Where the hell can we get a drink?' Oh dear.

And not easy. Tamil Nadu was a dry state. However Inkie explained that as non-Indians we might go to the District Collector's Office for our quota of liquor chits. So we did that, hung around there for ages in a queue which never shrank but I became restless and said 'Let's come back another time, I'll roll a joint,' and we wandered off to the St Stephen's Jumble Sale. Here a loose mix of residents were investigating the stalls, picking up, considering, price-asking, putting back, occasionally buying. I stirred the contents of a broken wheelbarrow, mostly old guidebooks, water-stained, worm-eaten, rat-gnawed, but I bought several including *The Indian Yearbook 1941-2*. This was an important publication. Its last four hundred pages comprised a living Who's Who of India at that time, an archive of extravagant characters, many accompanied by a photograph.

Rita was signalling. 'Darling, come and meet Dolores!'

Dolores said 'You can pay me for those books if you like.' She looked Anglo-Indian but said she was French and, as if to emphasise it, her jet hair was cut in a straight line below the ears with a square cut out for her face. 'How long are you here for?' she asked, 'and will you all come and have tea with us? We live over there.' Now and again when travelling, one comes across these engaging, spontaneous people – they're one's salvation really. So often, trying to bridge the gap with strangers is like greeting concrete, but Dolores was onto our case at once, and said 'Have you tried the coffee éclairs from the English Confectionery? You must.'

That evening at the Ratan Tata we smoked joints in the starry garden among scents of geranium, cypress and mildew. The Kashirs had gone but the greenish mechanical object in the sky was still with us and Sarah pondered 'So if it's not a star, and it's not a satellite, what on earth is it?'.

'For a start it's not on earth,' said Rita with a dry laugh. Mmm–we had to make more of an effort to find some booze.

Back inside in the main sitting-room there was a radio-gram the size of a coffin, with nets of gold metal over its loudspeakers, and we leafed through the records–Moura Lympany, Mantovani, Frankie Laine–but none was very tempting, so I withdrew to the bedroom and roamed through the potted biographies in *The Indian Yearbook*. There were hundreds of them: generals, princes, members of the Indian Civil Service, writers, politicians, and religious dignitaries. I was completely absorbed in this parade of Ruritanianism. One entry above all held my attention and I kept returning to it, perhaps because the postage-stamp sized photograph adjacent was so arresting. It portrayed a beautiful woman with passionate, sorrowful eyes. Her entry read as follows:

PAVRY, Miss Bapsy, M.A., Litterateur. *Educ*: Queen Mary High School and St.Xavier College, Bombay; M.A., Columbia University. Visited England every year since 1924. Presented at Their Majesties' Court, 1928; received by President Coolidge, by Pope Pius XI, by Signor Mussolini, by the Shah of Persia, and by the King of Afghanistan, by President Attaturk, by King Boris and Queen Joanna, King Carol and Queen Marie, Prince Regent Paul and Queen Marie of Yugoslavia, and the Crown Prince and Crown Princess of Italy, by Herr Hitler, King Leopold and Queen Elizabeth of Belgium, King George of Greece and King Farouk of Egypt, by President Lebrun [...etc...etc!]. *Publications*: Heroines of Ancient Persia (Cambridge 1930). *Address*: Malabar Hill, Bombay.

What a snapshot of an era. The two biographical entries following hers were of Miss Pavry's father and her brother. The brother, Jal Pavry, who described his career as 'Orientalist', had been received by the same gang of rulers. Obviously they'd gone in together, arm in arm. Unlike his sister, he had entered correctly in the singular Publication: *Zoroastrian Doctrine of a Future Life* (New York, 1926). But what on earth is 'an Orientalist'? Would anyone conceivably describe their career as 'an Occidentalist'? As for the father, Khursedji Pavry, he was a Zoroastrian high priest, 'First High Priest of the Fasali Parsis, elected 1920', who informs us in his entry that he has received 'dedications and tributes from many world-famous men.' Here in this family was a bizarre mixture of Zoroastrian fire worship, vulgar bombast, and international *grandeur*.

Did none of them have the slightest sense of humour? I longed to meet Miss Pavry and find out. If, that is, she were still alive; for in 1975, the world of the nineteen-twenties and -thirties was already another age. Afloat on the bed in a reverie, my mind recalled the words of Max Beerbohm concerning his visit to Algernon Swinburne in Putney (I couldn't remember the words precisely, but I've since then looked them up and they are: '...I was glad to see that he revelled as wistfully in the days just before his own as I in the days just before mine'). The thick volume of *The Indian Yearbook 1941-2* fell from my grasp, my eyelids sank, and I drifted asleep to the outlandish squawk of some restless creature on the other side of the window pane...

Lin's drive turned out to be more ambitious than expected and he turned out to be far more than a librarian – a game warden at a wildlife sanctuary, a keen calligraphist, a behavioural scientist, plant-lover, local historian. Wearing bwana shorts and boots, he collected us punctually in his jeep and we zoomed off to the kennels of the Ootacamund Hunt. This is the first and last of the Empire, in that it was the first hunt to be established on Imperial territory and is now the only one still at it, kept going these days by dandies from the Wellington Military Academy nine miles away. The hounds, seven couple, lined themselves up like washed and brushed schoolboys, wagging their tails for our camera. The gallop is over the Wenlock Downs in pursuit of jackals.

The Madras Government used to transfer to Ooty in the hot season and our next call was on Government House. 'Buckingham Castle it used to be called from having been established as an official residence by Richard Plantagenet Campbell Temple-Nugent-Brydges-Chandos-Greville, Duke of Buckingham and Chandos, when he was Governor of Madras,' said Lin and he paused to see what effect this celestial statement might have. I squirmed with almost erotic pleasure and made a note of it at once but Rita, I saw, was bending down, anxiously examining her rat-bite. The situation of Government House is choice, overlooking the town yet also sheltered, and approached through the

Botanical Gardens. But the House was more than locked up, it was sealed tight, its many windows cancelled by fawn blinds drawn down from within. There was not even a caretaker around, so complete was its embalmment. Passive and powerful, the building tantalised the imagination, and it seemed likely that were we to break open its heavy doors we should find that the British had not left India after all and were conducting therein an afternoon reception for local worthies, polite voices merging with the tinkle of teacups in shadowy, pillared drawing-rooms.

Lin looked about and barked 'No Todas!' The last of the Todas, a prehistoric tribe, are said to inhabit the Botanical gardens (which are extensive). But we saw nobody. Perhaps you have to stand and wait for a long time until they creep out, and Lin was impatient to crack on. Another prehistoric tribe hereabouts is that of the Badagas who in the past were famous for the superior quality of their opium, which they didn't smoke but ate formed into little squares of 'cavendish'.

As we drove from Mount Snowdon to Doddabetta Peak, Rita asked Lin 'Do you know Dolores?'

'Dolores Maclaine-Clarke?'

'Yes.'

'She hasn't paid her library subscription. I keep reminding her. Richard is very nice. She breeds Alsatians.'

That seemed the end of that, so I asked 'Have you heard of Bapsy Pavry?'

'Come again?'

'The daughter of a Zoroastrian high priest.'

'Oh. There are so many high priests around. Maybe my wife knows something.'

'You've got a wife?' asked Rita. She was surprised – and obscurely annoyed that he'd suddenly become less available.

'Yes, I have.' But he didn't elaborate.

Sarah asked him if he'd ever seen any UFOs. He hadn't. 'But I've seen an EFFO.' I think this was another colonial joke. (Am I being mean? I shouldn't be. Lin was so good to us. Dead now of course. God bless you, Lin.)

At Doddabetta Peak the view was rich with meadows and moorland, woods and plantations. One gasped. But Rita's rat-bite had swollen badly and was now filled with pus. Lin examined it. 'Not very nice,' he said. Rita whimpered and looked about with nervous eyes while Lin, muttering, searched in the undergrowth. Eventually he grunted with satisfaction, tore at a bunch of leaves, crushed them slightly and, applying them to Rita's calf, bound them in place with a strip of bandage from his first aid kit. 'You'll be fine now. Where would you like to go next?'

'To the Ooty Club. I need a cup of tea,' she implored.

'I'll drop you off. It's only a short distance from your hotel. You'll be able to walk back.'

'Aren't you joining us?' asked Rita.

'I'm not exactly welcome there.'

Fortunately we were. At the jumble sale we'd met its president, Jack Lawrence, who said 'Do come up'. The Ooty Club – snooker was invented there – occupies a low cream villa, with a portico of fluted ionic columns, at the top of a hillside covered with white lilies. It was very quiet. In the season it fills up, which pays for the rest of the year when it is almost empty. The regulars hate the season when the 'spivs' arrive. We met a spiv on the terrace, an early swallow, about twenty-five years old. He was dressed in a yellow polyester shirt and black drainpipe trousers, with a narrow silver tie and winkle-picker shoes. His head shone with coconut oil and above his lip was an inkline moustache, and hair grew out of his ears in wispy untended clouds.

Inside, squeaky-clean boys in gallooned ducks padded barefoot over the polished floors of teak beneath the smiles of many a martyred beast. Doors opened in all directions to other rooms revealing portions of chintz, pale Indian rugs, brass and sparkling glass. And the smell – oh, heavenly – of beeswax and flowers. Mrs Hill supervised the housekeeping, a chain-smoking drum majorette, short and plump. Despite her efficiency, or perhaps because of it, there was something slightly unhinged about her which wasn't dispelled when she told us her son worked in Aylesbury. Perhaps she was what a later age would call obsessive-compulsive.

'I live in Aylesbury!' exclaimed Rita, happy to have made this connection (she'd been looking for connections and not finding them).

A dark boy entered and asked me 'Will you take tea on the terrace, Master?'

Somewhat surprised by the mode of address, I pushed back my long curls and said 'Very nice, yes, thank-you.'

The only other person in the sitting-room was an ancient birdlike lady in the far corner. She lowered a copy of *The Financial Times*, combined a quick smile with arching eyebrows, and raised the *FT* again, shaking it into a papery roar. Her eyes, even across the room, were sea-green and her outfit drew on several civilisations in a manner we associate with the Ballets Russes: plum jacket and knickerbockers fastened below the knee, a blouse of oyster silk, a cream turban with a green toque held by a diadem, and patent shoes with silver buckles. Sleeping Beauty or Scheherazade?

The glassed verandah was alight with flame-coloured cushions inside and the profuse scarlet of geraniums outside. An English soldier and his wife, on leave from the Persian Gulf, were bewickered among the full panoply of tea. I asked the soldier 'Do you know who that extraordinary woman is inside?'

'Which extraordinary woman?'

'The one with buckles and feathers.'

'I think,' he ventured, 'it's someone called Queenie Wapshare.'

'I bet she knows Bapsy Pavry.'

'They say she knows everybody.'

'No, they say she's met everybody,' corrected his wife. 'It's not the same.'

'*Apparently,*' the soldier continued, 'the day India went off parity with Sterling she took up smoking again after thirty-six years. They say she met Queen Victoria as a child and that's why she puts on a German accent – in deference.'

'Does she have a German accent?'

'Didn't you speak to her?'

'No.'

'The BBC were filming here and she shot a coolie out of a fruit tree to show off.'

Something about the soldier – he didn't look absolutely solid. His thin, smart wife nibbled on a dry biscuit. 'I'm responsible for bringing Mervyn Peake to Muscat & Oman,' she said. 'They're all madly reading *Gormenghast* now in the desert. Would you like a sandwich?'

'This place is awfully good,' said the soldier.

'But I must say, I'd love a drink,' said his wife. We all agreed we'd love a drink but the bar wasn't open. I can't recall exactly how the liquor-allowance system applied to bars and hotels but I do know it wasn't straightforward. As for *Gormenghast* I can see how it might chime with readers who live in the Gulf, a region where, intellectually, the future is knocking ever more loudly on a worm-eaten door. A note preserved from this occasion says 'Sarah lit a cigarette and fixed her eyes upon a tureen of lilies'. Odd the things one sometimes jots down.

A couple of days afterwards we were provided with an even more copious tea at Dolores and Richard's. What I put in my notebook later was:–

'Collected by their good-looking driver in black Ford Zephyr. They live in a house called St Mary's at Fernhill, a little way past the mothballed Mysore Summer Palace. We were served three varieties of bread, five of jam, two of fruitcake, two of Madeira Cake, plus biscuits, on English china, with French silver, all heaving on a table of Kashmir walnut, and served by a relaxed and charming Indian footman. But the atmosphere in the house was disjointed. Richard was polite but in low spirits and did not join us at the table. He slunk out to the ferns of the greenhouse and played 78 rpm. records on his gramophone. One was Does the Chewing-Gum Lose its Flavour on the Bedpost Overnight. A mild, quiet man who must feel beached by history. The British ruled India but they did not colonise it. After independence virtually all the British left. Indians and Pakistanis subsequently came to Britain which they did not rule but which they colonised.'

Dolores flapped her hands expressively and said she was trying to write something about Sir David Ochterlony. 'I can't get going, I can't get going!'

I said what a wonderful name it was – presumably one of those Parsi names, or Sephardic Jewish names like Sassoon, but it turned out to be Scottish. Dolores said 'Spinach is a Parsi word.'

I thought Dolores could be Parsi but she didn't let anything slip. She said the name 'Bapsy Pavry' rang a bell.

'Ask Lin Townsend's wife – she's a Parsi.'

'Is she?'

'We've not met his wife,' said Sarah.

'No, she's kept in the background!' and Dolores laughed raucously.

'But my leg healed completely,' said Rita, rooting for him.

'Why isn't Lin welcome at the Club?'

'Because he sticks up our names in public for non-payment of library subscriptions. He stuck my name up! I was furious! Oh, let's have a wonderful dinner at the Club before you leave. I've been trying to persuade Richard to buy a house in Scotland. I think it's important for a man to have property in his own country, don't you?'

The driver dropped us back in the Zephyr. He was charming in a slightly cocky way and Lin told us afterwards that Dolores was in love with him. Inkie ran past us in the drive but stopped, jogging on the spot to say hullo. Rita said she'd heard there was a dance at the Military Academy at Wellington and Inkie, already out of breath, said 'I'll have to come back at you, dear lady, on that one.' Rita gave him a little wave as he lolloped past the lodge and into the lane for his exercise run. In that lodge lived a defunct Maharajah and his Welsh wife but we never saw them, not once. As for the Ratan Tata Holiday Home itself, it had originally been called Harrow-on-the-Hill and the property of a lady called Miss Cunliffe. You see how the lines of life branch out all over the place. But I shall have to resist going in quest of this long-dead Miss Cunliffe. I really would like to know who she was, how she came to live here, and what happened to her. Perhaps she was nobody and nothing happened to her, though instinct – or is it wishful thinking? – tells me that there is a curious story there too. Ah, yes, she gave birth to a mixed-race child who was sent to school in Singapore and Miss Cunliffe sought out her relations in Torquay but they didn't click and the mixed-race child, having become a wealthy businessman in Australia, bought a seaside flat for his mother in Sydney where she ended her days as the bridge partner of Lord Beauchamp, a man lately exiled from England in a homosexual scandal...

Booze chits became essential after all and Rita and I invested many hours in pursuit of the Liquor Permit for Temporary Residents and the various signatures and stamps it required. At last the final stamp and signature came down upon it and we were able to proceed. The only place where alcohol could be bought was Uttam's, the local department store. Excitedly clutching our permits, we passed through its menswear department – Suitings. *A Gay Selection in Terylene, Terycot, Terywool, and Nylon Bell-Bots. Modern Novelties of Woollen and All Kinds of Hosiery* – and upstairs through the women's department – *Sarees Exciting Wide and Fascinating Variety of Fabrics from All Over Indian*

Parts – to where in the distance a glass altar supported a pyramid of coloured bottles scintillant in the blood-red shafts of sunset. It was ten to six. We'd made it with only moments to spare. Rita and I collapsed into laughter at the relief and absurdity of it all, breaking at the knees, howling into walls, holding each other. The assistant was not in the leastly disconcerted – obviously this is a common reaction – and waited patiently with his head on one side, looking at us with shining eyes, smiling.

'What was that stuff you mentioned? Madras brandy, was it?'

'Yes, but it had a special name. I might recognise the bottle.'

She turned to the assistant. 'How much can we have?'

'One month's supply. Six bottles of spirits. Each.'

They were all Indian cognacs, whiskies, gins, etc. but turned out to be very tasty. As we left the counter bent by four carrier bags of alcohol, the assistant said 'Enjoy the party' with a modest wave. On the way back we diverted to St Stephen's churchyard, opened a bottle of plum brandy and had a slug beneath Indian oaks. Rita rapidly grew sentimental. 'Oh, darling, we should've invited that assistant to our party.'

'We're not having a party.'

'We should've invited him anyway,' she said. 'I'm sure he wanted to come.'

'I think he was just being nice.'

'Did you fancy him?'

'Yes, I did actually.'

'Oh lover of the Nile...' And she pulled my head into her comforting breasts, which was quite a habit of hers.

When we arrived back, Sarah said 'You're late' but we

fixed her a brandy & soda and she softened up.

Dolores made good her intention and on our last night we did dine with the Maclaine-Clarkes at the Club, bequeathing them our remaining bottles. Consequently we all got very drunk. But I do retain some faded notes and can piece it together.

The rendezvous was in Colonel Jago's Room, technically out of bounds to women but rules tumbled before the wild and sooty laughter of Dolores and the gentle chuckles of her husband – yes, Richard was almost lively. My toreador jacket and yellow bell-bots, which had gone down well at the Delhi Film Festival, went down well here too. Dolores introduced us to Brigadier Abkar ('an Armenian of the Calcutta shipping family' she explained sotto voce; I wondered later if the name was 'Akbar' but was told 'Definitely it's Abkar') whose own get-up was also quite snazzy. His bowtie bobbed, monocle flashed, and pale-blue eyes sparkled – he gave off such a terrific air of pleasure and screwed up his nose relishing our piquant use of language which was very modern to his ears. 'Order a dry martini. They're the best outside the Tollygunge,' he advised with a touch of self-mockery. His wife was adorable too – her gutturals rolled into laughter as she said 'We don't know Bapsy Pavry but we know about her!'

'You do? She looked very beautiful in her photograph.'

The Brigadier asked 'Would she choose an ugly photograph for *The Indian Yearbook*?' and he burst into laughter like a puppy.

I mentioned that my father had given me the address of a business contact of his who was a Parsi in Bombay and Richard said yes, that's where they were based and generally they were successful middle-class types. 'Originally the Parsis came from Persia,' he said, 'and had preserved their religion, Zoroastrianism, in pure form for three and a half thousand years. They worship fire and do not bury their dead but expose them on platforms for vultures to eat in a special place known as the Towers of Silence.' Richard could be very informative when encouraged.

'This special place is on Malabar Hill,' added the Brigadier, 'and quite near a small reservoir. After a while people got fed up with the vultures as they flew away dropping putrid human meat into the reservoir. Complaints were made and now I believe some sort of chicken wire has been placed over the reservoir to catch the bits.'

'But some would still fall through,' commented Sarah.

'Yes, I expect it would,' twinkled the Brigadier, 'but not so much.'

The Abkars couldn't stay for dinner – we tried to persuade them but they said the hour was too late. The dining-room was vaulted with black beams and set for a hundred. Fresh flowers were hopeful on every table but we were the only diners. Dolores said this was normal. We talked of language and I said 'When the Indians call me Master I feel marvellous. I haven't been Master since I was a boy.'

It was true, that being called Master gave one a really pleasant feeling – not of racial or class or gender superiority, but of superiority full stop, the sweetest simplest kind of uplift, as though a quiet blush were suffusing one's ego. It was flattery combined with a wish to be helpful. It's so important to receive compliments and therefore no less important to pay them. Many people are embarrassed by the idea of paying compliments – which is dreadful. We all need these boosts along the way. I remember once calling an old tramp 'sir' and he went into a transformation under my very eyes. Some chemical was released in him which hadn't been released maybe for years. And at a cocktail party in Mexico City the host said to me 'The trouble with the English is that they are suspicious of compliments.' He was right. The English tend to associate flattery with corruption, insincerity, and the lower forms of sexual seduction. They prefer charm. The trouble with charm is that only some people have it, whereas everyone can pay a compliment.

Of other forms of address, Sarah recalled that a gang of hooligans driving along in a banger had shouted to us 'Halloooo, my dears!' and Dolores said that 'my dear' was a widespread term of familiarity in the Nilgiris, even among hooligans. Inkie's adorable little son, in his school cap and satchel and grey socks, called his father 'sir' and me 'uncle'. I loved it when he called me 'uncle'.

Can't remember what food we ate that last night at the club but for some reason I got far more smashed than the others and lost it all in the gentlemen's washroom. Rita told me afterwards that one of the boys came to the table and said 'Excuse me, Madam, the Master is lying on the lawn,' and she'd replied 'Don't worry, he often does that.' A servant brought pudding out to me and laughed as he tried to persuade me to enjoy it. There were smears of stars and a brilliant moon but I don't recollect seeing the greenish mechanical object in the sky or even caring about it, though Rita later told me that she'd looked for it and it had gone. The lilies, masses of them cascading down the hillside, shone a fierce white. I do remember very well the astounding luminosity of those lilies, floodlit by the moon in the black Nilgiri night. Taking off my clothes and extending my full length I rolled from the top of the hill all the way down, crushing lilies as I went, wetting my naked body with cool lily juice.

DELUXE

About eighteen months after my return from India the strangest thing happened. Though I'd say I was a sensitive man, I'm not a great one for supernatural experiences. Anything odd I've usually been able to account for in relatively comprehensible terms. What now took place, however, I have never been able to explain away.

It began when I read in *The Times* newspaper an obituary under the headline 'The Dowager Marchioness of Winchester'. To my astonishment this woman turned out to be Bapsy Pavry. Well, well, well, along the way Bapsy had hooked a marquess – and not any old marquess either but the Premier Marquess of England. Well done, Baps. All of which was quite new to me. But I was very sorry she'd died. I'd missed the chance of meeting an unusual personality and listening to her colourful stories. I bet she was beautiful to the very end; she looked the type who would be.

At the time I was involved as a free-lance editor with a punk glossy magazine called *Deluxe* and I thought a piece on Bapsy would hit the spot. But when I came to research it I couldn't locate the Bapsy Pavry obituary. I thought I'd torn it out and kept it but, searching high and low without success, God knows what I'd done with it, so I thought I'd ask *The Times* to forward me a copy. After examining their records they reported back–to my great surprise–that no such obituary had been published by them. How odd... Maybe I'd befuddled the source? The nineteen-seventies were a befuddling period. Perhaps it had been in the *Telegraph*. When I contacted the *Telegraph* however, they said the same. Hadn't published an obit of Bapsy Pavry. I rang all the relevant papers and drew blank, blank, blank. No obits anywhere. This was perturbing and–well–had she in fact died? None of them had the foggiest idea. They didn't even know who she was.

This unnerved me. So I backtracked and tried to work it out. I'd read an obituary in the newspaper–but no obituary had been published – and it was of someone who would certainly have rated an obituary had she died–but editors seemed not to know of her existence–so maybe she hadn't died–so what had I read? Quite apart from the possibility of a phantom obituary, you'd think it a simple matter to ascertain whether or not a woman who'd been married to the Premier Marquess of England had died. Not a bit of it. I rang all possible authorities. No one knew whether she were alive or dead–and many didn't know of her at all.

Soon after this puzzle arose, I had lunch with John Betjeman. Which I *did* write up for *Deluxe*. The article incorporates the Reverend Gerard Irvine and his sister Rosemary who joined us at John's house before we left for the restaurant. The relevant portion of the article ran as follows:

DUNCAN: I had a very odd experience the other day. I read an obituary of Bapsy Pavry. Do you know her? I discovered her in *The Indian Yearbook* for 1942. Well, in this obituary I learned a lot more about her – that she had since become the Marchioness of Winchester, then the Dowager, how she'd made a full-scale assault on high society, got into trouble, and so on.

GERRY: She had a battle for the Marquess with Mrs Fleming.

SIR JOHN: Peter's mother.

ROSEMARY: And Ian's.

DUNCAN: Apparently Mrs Fleming sued her for alienation of her husband's affection. But the funny thing was that when I telephoned *The Times* for a copy of the obituary, they said they hadn't published one. No one else has either. So I phoned Nigel Dempster, the gossip columnist, and he said he'd last seen her alive and well at Ascot a few years ago. So where did that obituary come from which revealed to me new and accurate information about her?

GERRY: You should put it down now while you remember. We might be able to use it as an example of precognition. Her husband was the oldest marquess ever. He died at the age of a hundred or something.

SIR JOHN: Shall we go and eat?

I don't think Rosemary ever forgave me for calling her brother Gerry. She insisted that he was always called

Gerard. But I know that before they arrived, John had referred to him as Gerry and it stuck. The second thing I'd got wrong in the above was about Mrs Fleming sueing Bapsy – it was the other way round. The enormous row between Bapsy and Ian Fleming's mother was another whole limb of Pavriana I'd barely grasped. (Eve Fleming, widowed and very well-provided for when Valentine Fleming was killed in action in 1917, was subsequently one of the many mistresses of Augustus John and had a daughter by him.) Dempster also suggested I try the May Fair Hotel where sometimes Bapsy had lived. The May Fair made a search and said a woman of that name, either name, wasn't staying there and – inexplicably in the light of subsequent events – claimed to know nothing about her. Debrett's didn't know anything and the more thorough-going Burke's had ceased publication. I looked her up in my Burke's 1959 under 'Winchester'. That didn't say much except that her husband was born in 1862 and had married Bapsy in 1952, he aged almost ninety. I did later discover that the Marquess died at the Metropole Hotel in Monte Carlo in 1962, just short of his hundredth birthday. Nowhere could I discover *her* birthdate and couldn't recall it from the phantom obituary. I chanced across a second photograph of Bapsy, still the beauty, in Andrew Barrow's book *Gossip*. I think the photo was taken in the 1950s. But when I asked Andrew he couldn't add anything to that. It seemed an idea to write to the current Marquess of Winchester to ask the whereabouts of his 'kinswoman' – if that's the term. Reference books gave his address as 6a Main Road, Irene, Transvaal, South Africa. Oh God, another one who jumped ship. There was no reply.

Although the Bapsy story was getting more and more peculiar, my life was getting more and more complicated, and after several further shots at trying to discover whether or not she were alive, I gave it up as hopeless. The woman had vanished without trace.

SUCCESS

Nearly twenty years went by. Many things happened, including Rita's death. She died in her fifties from a stroke. It hit her in church while she was discussing the details of her mother's funeral with a priest. She keeled over in the aisle. And days later, in Stoke Mandeville Hospital where she'd been a much-loved hospital visitor, it was all over. This is not the place to write at length about her, except to mention that, after Ootacamund, Sarah and I accompanied Rita back to Sri Lanka; she returned to stay with the de Mels and we two took a room at a small hotel in Cinnamon Gardens and pursued our antics and intoxications.

The point about getting out of one's head on substances, especially in youth, is that things happen which otherwise wouldn't. One minute we were spending a night with Greek sailors on their ship Hyperion in Colombo harbour—all I remember is skidding across water and climbing up the side of a metal cliff; must've passed out because I came to in a small cabin roused by a big soft cock tapping gently against my cheek. The next moment we were on our way to the Oliphant Estate house at Newara Eliya where Rita was installed in a four-poster bed by the owner. Somewhere along the way we acquired a tall and handsome American called John who worked for the Peace Corps and rowed for Yale. When he joined us he was in straight clothes but by the time he left us he was talking to the birds in Kandy's Royal Botanical Gardens and wearing a sarong – so we did some good there I suppose.

But on other occasions Sarah and I must've been a pain in the neck, falling about like boneless banshees. Exorbitant behaviour was interposed with periods sitting, waiting, lying on beds, looking at ceilings, stranded, trying to organise money. Re-reading the letters to my parents (which they preserved), I'm horrified at how much of the content is about wheedling money out of them. The seductive trap was that one could live for months in these Third World places on a few hundred pounds. I supplemented this with reviews for an amused Frank Granville Barker at *Books & Bookmen* who loved the idea of posting a hardback volume to an Asian outback and eventually receiving a review some months later in fluorescent ink with twirly cartoons round the edge. Such material as the *Spectator* was able to publish supplied a little more cash – however my letter of introduction from the editor was more valuable for giving *entrée*. Officials at the British Embassy in Bangkok were so astonished that I should be a roving foreign correspondent for such a magazine that they rang the *Spectator* office in Gower Street. Gill Pyrah, who was editorial secretary at the time, picked up the phone and asked them 'Have you seen him wearing tight, bright-yellow flared trousers?' 'Yes, we have as a matter of fact.' 'Then that's Duncan.'

At the Fisherman's Inn in Galle, Sarah and I discovered that Robin Maugham, whom we were to meet, had moved on the day before. Galle was one of the hottest places I've ever been. The tropical gardens of the hotel were sticky with exuded juices and never caught even the slightest breeze. The sea itself was hot; at least that part of it was which we were able to access. We sat in the slurping, shallow wavelets of a cove wondering why we were there, but after a while even that question-with-many-answers was too precise. Lethargy flattened us.

Sarah and I took turns at reading *Fear and Loathing in Las Vegas* which I'd purchased at the Hotel Taprobane in Colombo. Its pages stored a vitality which had been entirely sucked out of our surroundings by the heat and we fought limply for possession of it. There were a couple of evening visits to the New Oriental Hotel in Galle Fort, where we sought solace beneath the fans and sat side by side staring into space with iced drinks in front of us. I can see now the condensation from those tall glasses soaking the tablecloth. Attempts to link up with Rita and her hosts were not successful. The de Mels were part of the political establishment and she was torn between looning with us and keeping us at arm's length. Rita was 'apart' in other ways. Where possible without offending the locals, Sarah liked to sunbathe topless, or naked in secret spots; I loved sunbathing too but, after burning my balls in Goa, usually dropped a little scarf over my bits. Rita however couldn't go into the sun at all. There was a generational difference too, not so much in years as in epochs. Sarah and I were in our mid-twenties but Rita was an older woman who'd had a straight married life before she knew us. We were 1960s kids, she'd been a 1950s girl. In the end a tough telegram from April Ashley told Rita to return to England and look after her four children. 'She's envious,' said Rita, which was doubtless true, but that didn't alter the facts – Rita had to go back.

Rita left Sri Lanka very unhappy with me and in due course I received letters from some mutual friends in England who wrote that I had been cruel to her. Before leaving she said to me 'Sarah's won'. But it wasn't true. Rita had got it all wrong. All of a sudden the person she wanted me to be, and thought I might become in a faraway paradise, had vanished off her radar – to be replaced in her mind by another person; that other person was equally fallacious but was more hurtful to her. Rita also knew that these weeks travelling with us was her last taste of freedom, that to return home to the care of her children and a job (in quality control for CBS Records) was *it*, was all she had to look forward to, the end of the dream of renewal. The melancholy of being left behind – by another, by events, by time itself – was made more difficult for her because she imagined me disappearing into an ever-fresh dawn with a rival. Sarah and I would have many more extraordinary experiences – the week following Rita's departure I would be in hospital in Madras after what the doctor called 'an infra-glauconic seizure' – before the two of us parted from each other in Bangkok, but we were never the couple which Rita's imagination had constructed.

Luckily I still possess the tiny Letts appointment diary I travelled with, which helps to resurrect those far-off days. And some weeks ago, sorting through a cupboard of old papers, I came across a notebook, written – and drawn (it has a lot of psychedelic drawings in it) – in the course of this meandering voyage which later took in Calcutta, Burma, Thailand, Laos and Penang. My God, the names of the pills it records are as exotic as the locations – Drinamyl, Soneryl, Nembutal, Durophet, Doriden, Tuinal, Desoxyn etc. I'll doubtless publish material from it, if I write a memoir of the nineteen-seventies, that wonderful wild decade which almost killed me. Its entries began in Galle, March 15th 1975, 6.30 pm, and make evident that the triangular adventure with the two women was causing me great difficulties too. Were we three running away from anything? Not really. It was more like we were running towards something – and it was more exciting when you didn't know towards what, because the important thing was to keep breaching the horizon, to enact the romantic idea of openness. If, as Coleridge said, the classical is the finite, then yes, this was the romance of travelling, the movement into a kaleidoscopic future continuously opening ahead of us. The fundamental problem of existence is infinity, that it is not possible to place limits on the infinite. All theory breaks down at that point, including that of curved space. So the finite can never harmonise one with reality. Only a sense of the infinite can do that. This was the pull.

Yet none of us was able to answer the needs of the other two. The notebook records my last night with Rita in Colombo. It was a Saturday and Sarah dropped out at the Intercontinental Hotel stage. 'Dinner Ceyfish Restaurant – Galle Face Hotel, gin and cakes – Mount Lavinia Hyatt, drinks over sea – Ceylon Intercontinental, cocktails and ice-creams – Samudra, Capricorn Nightclub to 4 am – Rita and me: smoking on beach – Galle Face Hotel, breakfast 6.30 am. Mind in a mess of drugs, sentimental departure chat (Rita says "I don't think I'll see you again for a long, long time"), intense feelings of fatigue and God knows what.'

I'd hurt Rita without realising how much I'd hurt her. Yet though I couldn't be what Rita wanted me to be, I never blanked her. If once you enter the arena of intimacy with someone, you owe them honest explanations to the best of your ability. You must never blank people when intimate relations have arisen; you must never slam the door in their face. I've been the victim of it several times – and it's the worst. It gives you no chance of dealing with it and working it through. You just stand there in the middle of the road wondering what happened, what did I do. Rita couldn't really talk about it in India or in Sri Lanka because we were three. But we talked about it afterwards back in England, we sorted it out, and remained close friends. You can sort things out if only you talk honestly. Honesty is the key. That's another thing Rita taught me, one of the most important lessons in life: how not to be shy of the heart. So many people can't talk about what they feel. So they stew and hide and everyone gets muddled up. But if Rita had 'got me wrong', I could never shake off the feeling that in many ways she knew me better than I did myself. This was part of her hold on me and fascination and purpose: her emotional intelligence.

OK. So one evening I was chatting to a stranger in the Champion pub in Notting Hill Gate. It turned out he was a barrister and his name was James Pavry.

'Really?'

'Yes, really. Why, shouldn't it be?'

'Do you happen to be related to someone called Bapsy Pavry?'

'I think I am, yes.'

'Do you know what happened to her?'

'No, I don't think I do. In fact I'm sure I don't. We lost contact with her years ago. I presume she died. She was very old even at that time. You should ask my brother – he knows more about that sort of thing. Have you seen her portrait?'

'No. Where?'

'It's by Augustus John and hangs in the Royal Academy. You should go and look at it.'

So I did. It hung in the gallery of the Norman Shaw staircase near the restaurant. The portrait of Bapsy was vivid and strangely aloof, the face pale and red-lipped, the eyes almost on the verge of tears. Her mass of black hair was partly covered by the drape of a cream sari. A woman of contradictions. And like its subject, the portrait was unreachable. One could view it across the deep stairwell but not get any closer because the gallery where it was placed had been permanently closed to the public. And to-day it is not on view at all, presumably packed away somewhere in the dungeons, too much of an inexplicable thing in the Royal Academy's glassy new world of blockbusters and gift shops.

When I rang James Pavry's brother, he knew nothing and asked 'How did you come to be interested in her?'

As I gave him the outline, soft velvet curtains opened on the interior stage of my memory and additional scenes from the nineteen-seventies presented themselves. I recalled that the Abkars at Ootacamund had said that they knew *about* Bapsy Pavry, but I'd been too pissed to pursue it. Presumably they were dead now. But I thought I'd take up the matter again with Richard and Dolores Maclaine-Clarke; after my return from India we had exchanged Christmas cards for a few years but the contact fizzled out. In case they'd moved, I wrote to them care of the Ooty Club.

Not long after – in December 1994 – I was sitting with my friends Von and Keith in a restaurant in Kensington Church Street called Boyd's which isn't there any more (restaurants do come and go with great frequency). Half-way through dinner I was telling them of my twenty-year quest for Bapsy Pavry, when an old lady in black, looking Indian or Anglo-Indian, walked past our table on the arm of a page-like boy. White crystal brooches glittered on her black straw hat. She had an air of great distinction but was at the same time very much a fish out of water.

'That could be her, the very one,' I whispered excitedly.

'Go after her,' urged Keith. 'Ask her if she's Bapsy.'

'Do you think so?'

'Look, you're losing her, be quick, go on!'

I was on the point of following when the old lady faltered and almost fell down the step. She was salvaged by the boy but there was minor commotion and it was enough to inhibit me. Soon they were climbing into a cab and were gone. Had the long arm of synchronicity touched us? Was this Bapsy's last outing?

James Pavry recurred – he turned out to be a friend of old friends of mine, Simon and Jenny Willans, and when I saw him at Jenny's fortieth birthday party, I said that I'd had no luck with his brother and asked him about the Parsis.

'Actually my family became Roman Catholic but there are quite a lot of Parsis in London. Since she was the daughter of a high priest, they should know something.'

Under 'Parsi' in the phonebook there was nothing. I tried 'Parsee'. Like 'sari' and 'saree', the two spellings are interchangeable. But again nothing. I tried Zoroaster, Zoroastrianism. Nothing. I rang India House. After numerous transfers I spoke to a Mr Vadya who told me to contact a Mr Rusi Dalal, President of the Zoroastrian Trust Funds of Europe, at his home in Ealing. When I rang Mr Dalal, his wife told me he wasn't in, but she said he would be in later and he would ring me. I knew what that meant – nobody rings back any more. But I was wrong and he did.

'Mr Dalal!'

'Yes, sir. How can I help you?'

'I'm trying to find out about someone called Bapsy Pavry.'

'You are talking about Marchioness?'

'You know!'

'Indeed. We were looking after her.'

'You were? Is she dead?'

'No.'

'No?'

My God – no. She's alive.

'And you know where she is?'

'Yes.'

Finally...

'She was here until very recently,' he went on. 'But she is very old. You know that one – not best of health. She has just gone to Bombay and has asked us to make certain arrangements. She said she won't be back. You understand.'

'Yes.'

Mr Dalal sounded a lovely man. His manner of

speaking reminded me very much of Krishnamurti's.

'But if you are interested in such a lady, there was here a Lady Bomanjee, wife of a Parsi baronet. She died in Harrogate and they declared a public holiday. Her daughter is a Nehru and greatly revered. Miss Nehru is still here. In Harrogate.'

'Thank-you very much. But really it was Bapsy Pavry I was hoping to find. And since she is still alive, um, I could go to Bombay, couldn't I? How old is she?'

'Well over ninety years of age. I don't want to be discouraging, not at all, but – I wouldn't barge in if I were you. She might not be in fit state. You understand what I mean? I was in Bombay for a few days not long ago, but I didn't call there.'

'Might I send her a letter through you?'

'Yes, yes, of course, that would be the wisest course of action. But please don't misunderstand; I wish to help in any way.'

'Can I ask you another question?'

'Please do.'

'Do Parsis practice circumcision?'

'It's optional.'

What a nice religion it sounds.

THE OBITUARY

I wrote a letter to the Marchioness requesting an interview, Mr Dalal wrote back to me saying he'd forwarded it, and we waited. During the wait I discovered a little more – that 'paradise' and 'magic' are Persian words and that Bapsy had been spotted at receptions at India House hiding sandwiches inside her sari. 'She was so poor,' said my Indian informant mischievously, 'that she scavenged them to eat later. She married the Marquess thinking he was rich and he married her thinking she was rich and they were both disappointed.'

In July of 1995 I received a reply from the Secretary of the Ootacamund Club, Mrs Patel, saying 'I regret to inform you that both Mr and Mrs Maclaine-Clarke passed away some years ago.' Oh...so he never did buy that property in Scotland, and Dolores was so jolly one can hardly imagine her succumbing to anything. Because I didn't witness their decline, for me they will always be alive, he shy and quiet, she cackling away on the verandah of the Ooty Club for all time...

It was now that the second climax in this weird story took place. The Swiss photographer Luca Zanetti and myself were on the 16.10 train from Mallaig to Glasgow. Mallaig is on the west coast of Scotland and we were returning from our search for a German artist called Maruma (and the story of that will be recounted in the next chapter). The point here is that at the kiosk in Mallaig I'd bought a bunch of newspapers and upon opening *The Times* (September 7th 1995), there it was staring at me. The same lay-out, the same headline, the same photograph, that very obituary which somehow I had seen, glimpsed, dreamed, conjured up so many years before. The Dowager Marchioness of Winchester, it said, had died in Bombay on September 6th at the age of ninety-three. The first climax had been the discovery she was alive; the second that she was dead.

WHAT FOLLOWED

Other obituaries soon appeared. Most were patronis-
ing and written in a tone of dry ridicule. But information
started to flow and I was able to put together more of the
story. It turned out that stealing sandwiches at receptions
was not out of necessity but from frugality. Bapsy at the
time of her death had been well-off and had made numerous bequests–to the universities of Oxford and Bombay,
for example, to good causes and religious groups. Many
of these offerings were dedicated to the memory of her
brother Dr. Jal Pavry. But the obituarists had made it obvious that she and her brother both before and after the
Second World War had been a kind of double act, seeking
advancement in London society by serving on charity committees and writing letters to titled and influential persons.
In Bapsy's case this went beyond snobbery and became
a lust for self-aggrandisement, a high romantic passion
capable of crossing into the absurd; on occasions she was
importunate, maddening, pitiful. Paradoxically that zeal-
ous and lifelong campaign to put herself on the world map
had had the contrary result–and she'd disappeared. People
had learned to see her coming and deflect her before she
arrived. Oh, I wish I'd been able to meet her. All those
years searching and there she was, somewhere in Ealing,
longing to be brought out of her dark corner and into the
light again.

Bapsy's great triumph was her marriage to the Marquess–and despair followed almost at once. Such an
abrupt reversal of fortunes can plant a deep and destruc-
tive rage, leading to years of incomprehending obsession.

You meet someone – and if it's the right person it is always unexpected. One can never scheme for meeting the right person. It is always by chance, an accident, but you know it's the special one because suddenly life throbs with colour and opportunity and meaning. Your deepest needs are fulfilled. You have everything. You're in heaven. Seconds later – it seems only seconds – that 'someone' closes their heart to you. The vistas vanish. All is cancelled. None of it makes sense. But you are in Siberia. You spend the rest of your life trying to grasp what on earth happened, or poisonously seeking redress.

Not only was Henry Winchester very old – Bapsy's father-in-law was born in 1801! – but he'd gone bankrupt in 1930 and had lived more or less hand-to-mouth on the Riviera ever since, trading on his title. In the year following their marriage, the Coronation of Elizabeth II loomed. Henry, for reasons of health or problematic relationships, decided not to attend. Bapsy was mortified. The Coronation? Not go? If she couldn't budge her husband, she'd go alone...But the Earl Marshal denied her permission to attend in her own right – it was one of Bapsy's bitterest moments. Next thing Eve Fleming moved in with Monty (Henry Winchester was often known as Monty) at the Metropole Hotel – what a blow. How had that come about? Well – Mrs Fleming had in fact been engaged to Monty in 1951. But she'd broken it off for fear of losing the widow's stipend which had enabled her to live very well. So the following year, in a hope or a huff, we'll never know, probably a mixture of the two, that's what it usually is, mixed motives, only a zombie can be truly single-minded, let us say then on the rebound, Monty married Bapsy at Caxton

Hall in London. How exactly she'd met him and how precisely the marriage had come about I was unable to fathom. But the old boy continued (as one would expect) to keep his hand in with Eve Fleming. Why Eve should have wanted to keep her hand in with him is yet another mystery. It can't have been the title because that had already gone to her rival. It can't have been love-making prowess unless Monty was an utterly different man when his clothes were off, which seems unlikely. Eve actually claimed 'Our association was as pure as an Easter lily', and one suspects that sadly there was no alternative. Perhaps it was Mrs Fleming's sheer cussedness. Anyway there she was, shacked up with another woman's marquess at the Metropole where they occupied separate rooms.

Bapsy made repeated sorties down to Monte Carlo and tried to entice, cajole, bully her husband back. Monty, sheepish, and wondering whether or not he'd done the right thing by either women, nonetheless avoided recapture by his legitimate spouse, and after a few months Bapsy was rumoured to be threatening divorce. In 1953 Monty, wrapped in a blanket, was carted off by Eve Fleming to Emerald Wave, her home at Cable Bay in the Bahamas. Bapsy retreated briefly to India but soon emerged and flew to the Caribbean in her most glowing saris to pace the road outside Eve's villa, shaking her fist at it.

Eve wrote to or rang her fashionable friends, saying 'that dreadful woman is stomping up and down outside my house, shaking her fist at us.' The fashionable friends duly noted it in their diaries for posterity. So far Eve was several laps ahead. But Bapsy took the matter to court, accusing Eve of enticing her husband away, and wrote vitriolic letters to Monty who seemed quite detached from the whole thing, merely content to have some woman with a nice house take care of the bills. 'May a viper's fangs be for ever around your throat,' the Marchioness wrote to her husband, 'and may you sizzle in the pit of your own juice!' The case came to a head in 1957 and the judge found in favour of Bapsy, but the following year in the Court of Appeal the judgement was reversed. Since Cable Bay had now been sold, perhaps to pay legal fees, Monty and Eve withdrew to the Metropole Hotel (charmingly down-at-heel in the 1950s) for the rest of his life. Monty Winchester died in 1962, aged 99; Eve Fleming died two years later, not quite 80. What an agonising humiliation for Bapsy it had been.

Then my agent of that time, Gillon Aitken, rang with another snippet of information. He'd read in the *Daily Telegraph* that Bapsy Pavry had left her papers to the City of Winchester. Naively she'd believed that in England, as in India, there was a fundamental connection between the holder of a title and the place of the title, but of course this had generally ceased to be the case hundreds of years beforehand. Embroiled in altogether different events in St Petersburg, I was unable to pursue Gillon's lead until the autumn of 1996 when I rang Winchester Town Hall. They put me through to a Mrs Brisbane, an American, who said 'Yes, we have the Marchioness's archive here. Come and have a look. You're the first person to ask.'

'Is there loads of stuff?'

'There are nine large cardboard boxes containing various things.'

On what turned out to be the wettest and windiest November day in Lord knows how many years, I steamed down to Hampshire in the car and found an hotel not far from the city. It was called the Marwell Safari Lodge and they put me in the Gazelle Pavilion. Outside the rain turned to sleet.

WINCHESTER 1996

The city of Winchester had greatly changed since last I was there. That had been over thirty years previously, while still at school, when during the summer holidays I was touring cathedral cities with a friend. In those days Winchester was still coherent architecturally but, like so many historic towns, it has since been broken up. Its City Council offices for example must be quite the nastiest in the whole of England, modernism degraded to a big dead lump. Fortunately Bapsy Pavry's archive was not housed there but in a group of old houses called the Historic Resources Centre. Yesterday's downpour had cleared to a sunny sky, with a bitter wind driving down from the north, and crows brayed from the gables as I entered this quaintly huddled facility.

The first shock came when Mrs Brisbane asked 'Do you know about her Will?'

'No, I don't.'

'She left the City of Winchester quite a lot of money.'

'Really? How much?'

'Something in the nature of a million pounds.'

'Good God.'

'It was agreed before she died. It's supposed to be used for the creation of a memorial hall with her name on it. But we've got enough halls.'

'You should have told her that before agreeing to take the money.'

'It's certainly a knotty problem. The photocopier's over there if you want to copy anything.'

The problem of the bequest was compounded by the fact that Bapsy's precise conditions on the gift had been determined many years before, during her one and only visit to Winchester in 1955. Subsequently a fire in the Guildhall destroyed the relevant records and the Mayor was too embarrassed to ask her to repeat the conditions. The Council still hoped to get the money without having its hands tied, just as it also accepted the gift of her portrait by Frank Salisbury but hid it away. Bapsy was right to place conditions on her gift. As the destruction of much of Winchester proves, the Council has a distressing record of philistinism. Not long ago, in order to create a car park, the Council intended to demolish the graceful Peninsula Barracks at the top of the town, designed in part by Christopher Wren, until a high-profile campaign by the pressure group SAVE blocked the bulldozers. The Barracks have since been converted into flats which are highly sought after and the whole compound become a great adornment to the city.

Mrs Brisbane took me through several low vestibules to a long oak table. The nine cardboard cartons of Bapsy's archive were waiting beside it on the cold floor and Mrs Brisbane explained what they variously contained. I thanked her, sat down at the table, took a deep breath, and leaned into the first big box. With source documents it's no good being hasty. You have to slow right down, sift in a systematic yet leisurely manner, allow yourself to be absorbed by another world. I'd brought along a stack of ham & mustard sandwiches for the duration.

The material was divided broadly into documents and objects. The documents had been subdivided into large envelopes by year and began chronologically with an invitation to a Buckingham Palace garden party on June 25th 1924. Most of the letters were on coroneted paper with red, blue or green borders, sometimes black for mourning, and were nearly all replies from notables to initiatives from Bapsy. Many were thank-you's for being sent either her own book or her brother's book or both; among the fortunate recipients were Tagore, G. B. Shaw, several Archbishops of Canterbury, the Maharajah of Kapurthala, the Maharajah of Jaipur, the Aga Khan, Queen Mary, the Duchess of York, the President of France, Neville Chamberlain, the Viceroy of India, the Crown Prince of Saudi Arabia, Cornelius Vanderbilt, and John D. Rockefeller, Jr.

The charity ball committee, then as now, was a route for female social advancement (men on such committees are 'suspect') and here one discovered Bapsy helping out the British Empire Cancer Campaign at the Dorchester Hotel, or the National Children Adoption Association 'do' at the Grosvenor House Hotel. Edwina Mountbatten, Loelia Westminster and the Countess of Athlone could always rely on Bapsy and her brother to sell tickets for these heart-rending fundraisers. One saw too copious evidence of another of Bapsy's ploys for penetrating the *monde*: whenever she read in the paper of anyone important suffering a bereavement, she would fire off a letter of condolence and would thereafter sweep into the memorial service like an old friend of someone who was usually a complete stranger to her. Royal film premieres start to feature in the nineteen-thirties but her attempts to claw her way further into royal circles were adroitly blocked:

Letter from the Lord Chamberlain, Lord Cromer, 6th June 1937

Dear Miss Pavry,
In answer to your letter of Dec 11th which reached me recently I am writing to say that as you were presented at Court in 1928 this presentation stands, and no re-presentations are made on the occasion of a new Sovereign; while Summonses to court are restricted to married ladies desirous of making presentations.
                    Yours sincerely,
                    Cromer

By 1930 Bapsy was living at the May Fair Hotel in Berkeley Square and paying visits to the USA (usually to Washington) or to India. Officially the family still lived at Sunama House in Bombay's posh residential district of Malabar Hill where most of the grand villas have since been destroyed.

Here is an example of the best sort of invitation which would arrive at Sunama House: 'The Aide de Camp in waiting is commanded by His Excellency the Viceroy to invite Miss Bapsy Pavry and Dr Jal Pavry to an Investiture to be held at "The Viceroy's House" New Delhi on Saturday the 27th of February 1937 at 9.20 pm. Full dress.' What a funny time of day. 9.20 pm. The Empire abounded with such apparent eccentricities but there was always a seed of logic behind them. Obviously after dinner.

On April 9th 1939 a great anniversary would come to pass. Her father who was, you recall, a Parsi High Priest of some arcane description, was going to reach eighty years of age. Rulers across an unsuspecting globe were informed of this in advance by a large mail-out from brother and sister, and the secretaries of many heads of state duly responded with letters of congratulation, all carefully filed here. In a world of good manners it is amazing what pushy people can achieve.

There's a bit of a gap in the archive 1940-46. She was staying for the Second World War mostly at the Taj Mahal Hotel in Bombay, where Sarah Moffett and I stayed (though the floor manager disapproved of us and our hippy attire and showed great ill-temper if ever we asked him anything, once even shouting insults at us across the main foyer). Not long ago the hotel was subjected to a murderous assault by Islamic terrorists and I noticed on the television pictures that the hotel's once airy interior spaces have been clogged up with little shops.

Singapore fell but India held, and Bapsy's box reveals that, though other invitations were thin on the ground, the viceregal garden parties continued ceremoniously throughout the war–'Morning dress or Lounge suits'. But the social round doesn't gear up properly again until the Aga Khan's Weighing Against Diamonds ceremony in March 1946 at the Bombay Cricket Club. This was taken to be the social event which signalled back-to-normal and soon the old routine is in full swing.

And on and on it goes. The universe may change but

not the pattern of Bapsy's life. The May Fair Hotel's beautiful premises in Berkeley Square had been demolished before the war (on the eastern side where Horace Walpole's house stood – that came down too) to be replaced by plain brick showrooms. The hotel moved to a new, characterless building in Stratton Street, and Bapsy moved with it; followed by winter at the Washington Hilton or in Bombay. I looked up the year I thought I read the phantom obituary – 1977. Empty envelope. Nothing in the archive. Very appropriate.

On turning to the boxes of objects, I had to cope with a vast trove of gimcrack rubbish: medallions, pins, salvers, tickets to Ascot, scrolls recording her and her brother's degrees from Columbia University in New York, delegate-badges to vainglorious international conferences, keys to cities which she'd purchased at souvenir counters, signed photographs from the Kings of Arabia and Morocco, of Belgium, Bulgaria, Greece and Italy, from sundry Popes and astronauts, from Mary Pickford, President Nehru, the Nizam of Hyderabad, the Emperor of Ethiopia, the Crown Princess of Japan, Éamon de Valera, Stanley Baldwin, the Windsors, Presidents Eisenhower, Nixon, Reagan and Bush, Margaret Thatcher, Dan Quayle...Dan Quayle? Remember him? I don't.

It was queasily fascinating – no – more than that – it was horrible and nauseating, this discrepancy between the pitch of her ambition and the banality of the result. Bapsy must have been so personal and ingratiating in her approach; the secretarial responses are so pleasantly impersonal. Yet what more could she expect? It was not that she merely wanted to associate with the great, it was that her whole life was a campaign to become one of the great figures of the age, and doomed on that account, because she never really did anything except social-climb. You can't be great by association. And what, I wondered, had happened to the truly personal correspondence and photographs? Letters to and from real friends. Photographs of family members or kindred events. Did she destroy them or did she never have any? Living in hotels, did she have no private circle, no domestic world? Her brother died in 1985 but there is nothing of him here, not a snap, not a note, nothing. And no bank records for her, no medical or hotel or shopping bills. Nothing intimate. And nothing of Bapsy herself. Nothing in her voice. Not a single letter of Bapsy's own anywhere, not even carbon copies. Just a stack of replies to what must have been received by public figures with embarrassment. The whole thing was pathetic really.

The only personal letters retained in the archive are a small number she received from Monty Winchester, the husband, who signs himself 'Henry'. In October 1952 he is writing from the Metropole Hotel to Bapsy at the May Fair – Monty wants a simple funeral when the time comes, he wants to be cremated, and the ashes are to be placed in the family vault at Amport. In January 1953 he's writing 'My darling Bapsy…I am the luckiest man in the world to have the most wonderful wife in the world. Your devotion, loyalty and love and affection have made my life the happiest ever…' And that's it. No mention of Mrs Fleming or law suits or divorces.

But Monty's abrupt and above all *unexplained* switch to the other woman, unexplained to Bapsy, that is, was to destroy her peace of mind for ever. When the other party has a change of heart but will not tell you why they have, or indeed that they have – this is the cruellest mystery of all, for the mind cannot rest but cogitates ceaselessly. What happened to turn warm to cold and yes to no? Why am I suddenly repulsive? Is it something I am or was it something I did? Who whispered what into your ear? Were there other circumstances I don't know about and which could enable me to forgive you, or you to forgive me? People who lead others up the garden path and then vanish and offer no reason, they are, well, it's difficult for callousness to get any lower. Where there was contact they create an abyss. In place of meaning they offer darkness, in place of understanding only an anxious and corrosive questioning of the empty air. In court she would say later that she felt as though her husband had 'murdered' her. The Marquess did this, as so many do, by hiding behind good manners and feebleness, assuring her against all the evidence of his actions that he was still devotedly hers. In this instance, for all her vulgarity, absurdity, and naivety, I am entirely on Bapsy's side against that withered old shit Monty.

Nonetheless Bapsy had been quick to exploit her apotheosis as the Premier Marchioness of England. Given the tenor of the replies, it is not difficult to divine the gist of what her own letters must have contained. Only days after her marriage, she is pestering the Chester Herald at the College of Arms over what she should wear for the Coronation of Queen Elizabeth II. The reply is a polite be-patient. Knowing what we know, subsequent letters on the same subject from the Bluemantle Pursuivant of

Arms at the Earl Marshal's office in Belgrave Square are poignant indeed:

10th December 1952

Dear Lady Winchester,
I have to inform you that it would be quite in order for you to wear a Sari underneath your Kirtle and train if you attend the Coronation. I must, however, add that in the event of your wearing a Sari it should be of white or cream coloured material with silver or gold but no colour.

But she wanted more.

1st January 1953

Dear Lady Winchester,
Thank you for your letter to me in reply to mine...The wearing of a tiara is optional although it is hoped that most Peeresses will wear one. I must point out, however, that the wearing of the Coronet will be obligatory and that it should be borne in mind that it can be put on only after the Queen has been crowned, and must therefore be done without the aid of a looking-glass. I hope you will not mind my pointing this out to you but you might find some difficulty in doing this if the Sari is draped over your head;
I must leave this to your own ingenuity.

Those Bluemantle Pursuivants of Arms think of everything – though it's rather creepy to find one of them so assiduously at work on New Year's Day. With estrangement from the Marquess on her mind, Bapsy's attempts to avoid being marginalised turned to panic. Repeatedly she badgered the Earl Marshall's office to be included in Royal or State occasions or indeed in any occasions whatsoever. The Earl Marshall's secretary from 1954 was Richard Graham-Vivian, who had been Bluemantle Pursuivant of Arms in the nineteen-thirties. He was the cousin of Evelyn Waugh's boyfriend Alastair Graham (of whom much more in chapter four) and Graham-Vivian showed great skill in neutralising her appeals without either giving offence or giving an inch. If protocol or her harassment of them allowed no way out, courtiers would resort to the time-honoured snub of sticking Bapsy behind a pillar at the occasion into which she'd forced her way. Barbara Cartland too was sometimes on the receiving end of that one, for example at the marriage of her step-granddaughter Diana Spencer to the Prince of Wales.

It is remarkable to relate but the last Bapsy box – the nineteen-eighties and nineteen-nineties – shows virtually no difference from the first box in the nineteen-twenties, except that in the absence of an Indian Viceroy, the Royal factor proper has gone up. Letters to all members of the British Royal Family on their birthdays are politely and affably answered by courtiers (who are well trained in this tedious task and have been accustomed to huge quantities of unsolicited communication throughout history). And the poor darling is still sending out copies of her one and only book; for that singular gift, thank-yous arrive from the Library of Congress, the Royal Geographical Society, Harvard University. One only wonders why these august bodies had not received their copies donkey's years before. Perhaps they had.

Bapsy's breathtaking resilience, her social crudeness, her absolute refusal ever to pick up a dropped hint, also keep her up to snuff on the London-Bombay-Washington round. She has already for many, many years been writing to the children or grandchildren of the people she used to write to, expressing sorrow and sympathy over their parents' or grandparents' demise. By now Bapsy was surreal, monstrous, an ineradicable constant and risible hanger-on in a rapidly changing world. In this final box the replies from persons-in-waiting or secretaries to members of the British Royal Family outnumber all the other letters in it: she'd become a crank who, judging from the unfailingly courteous apologies often contained in these letters, frequently wrote again if the answers were insufficiently prompt or grovelling. And all the while, as I squirrel through the cardboard cartons at the oak table, there hangs on the wall at my back an aerial photograph of Winchester city before the terrible demolitions began, to remind one of the glorious streets which have been ravaged or altogether lost.

For the year 1992 there is recorded a donation by Bapsy of £24,000 to Oxford University, founding two awards in international peace and understanding, in memory of her and of her brother. What happened to the awards? I've never heard of any such award. I must write to whomever you write to about such things. Perhaps I could snaffle one for this piece you're reading. Not that twenty-four grand would generate much. A thousand quid per annum max? That's all right, even to-day. I could have great fun with a thousand quid. Oh dear, I hope Bapsy's not contagious – her heckling for responses, answers, resolutions. In life one can't have all the answers. There are always more questions. If you push it, everything peters out in questions in the end. And all this 'in memory of'; she had no children of course or serious reputation or other form of perpetuity.

On December 26th 1992 Bapsy was ninety years old; the letters of congratulation from the Royal Family downwards are all in reply to those from her informing them of this triumphant anniversary. And the one unsolicited person in the whole world who was trying to find her – me – couldn't! If only I had a handle to my name, her nose would've tipped up in the air and by infallible instinct she would have been on to me within the hour. This birthday also means that *The Times* obit had it wrong; she was not 93 but still only 92 when she died. Unless she'd decided to give herself an official birthday as well as a real one, choosing in the former case to follow Jesus by twenty-four hours. Bapsy is last registered at the Washington Hilton in 1993, and she received correspondence at the May Fair Hotel up to 1994. This is incredible really, that she kept it up for so long, even with two passports. She was obviously one of those double-passport people, which I've never been. They're getting more and more common, aren't they, the double-passport people. I've never knowingly met a triple-passport person but having three passports, that's probably a rapidly increasing genus too. Like so many misfits, Bapsy was a pioneer. As for her madcap social behaviour, it was tailor-made for the internet: lots of clicks, little substance, and all smeared into a personal fantasy of self.

Then to Bombay for the fade-out. It is in that great Victorian city of her birth that she receives the final letter in the archive. It is from Clarence House and is dated 31st of January 1995, the year of Bapsy's death, and after all that exasperated and exasperating correspondence, something a little more personal, a little more real:

Dear Lady Winchester,

I am writing in reply to your letter to the Lady-in-waiting and to Queen Elizabeth. [Can I interrupt a second? Buckingham Palace told me that this refers to the Queen Mother, since in official correspondence Queen Elizabeth II is always just 'the Queen'. Bapsy forms a valiant triumvirate with the Queen Mother and Barbara Cartland as women who *lived* the century.] I have had the opportunity of giving your letter to Her Majesty and I am to say that she was very distressed to hear of your long illness and to know that you are unable to leave your room. Queen Elizabeth remembers with pleasure the letters you have sent her over the last 62 years, and has asked me, on her behalf, to send you her very best wishes and her hopes and prayers that the future will bring you peace. May I add my own wishes too, as I remember you well at my wedding in 1950, when my maiden name was Elphinstone.

Yours sincerely,
Margaret Rhodes.

How happy this letter must have made Bapsy, the personal wave at last from the great world she had never really entered, coming as it did from the fount of all feminine nobility and belonging and influence, from none other than Elizabeth the Queen-Empress herself, wife of George VI, the last King-Emperor of India. With impenetrable Indian ink, Bapsy has obliterated the Bombay address it was posted to. Her final abode must have been insufficiently glamorous for posterity's eyes. But that last letter reminds us how by taking a little trouble now and again, by thinking a little about the other without any great inconvenience to oneself, by daring to be simple and truthful and well-mannered, one can cancel a void, and bring ease and delight where there was uncertainty and pain. Margaret Rhodes had accomplished more than she knew with that friendly, humane touch; or perhaps she did know, which is why she had the job.

Mrs Brisbane, the Winchester archivist, poked her head round the door. 'Finished?'

'Yes, thank-you.'

'Do you want to see the portrait?'

'I don't think so.'

'It's a big gaudy thing. We don't know what to do with it.'

'I think I've finished.'

But not quite. *The Indian Yearbook* entry on her father – I'm looking at it now – said that he had three sons and three daughters. Bapsy must have had family back in Bombay, plenty of family, even though not a jot in the archive makes any mention of them. I rang Mr Dalal. He said 'She took everything back to Bombay except the material she donated to Winchester.'

'You don't know if any other papers exist?'

'I'm afraid I don't.'

'And what about her family – cousins, nieces, nephews?'

'I'm not sure of the family set-up. But I'm going to Bombay soon and can ask for you. She was going to donate money to us for a library but placed so many conditions on it that we couldn't accept. The main stumbling block was that she said the room had to be named after her. I explained that at Zoroastrian House we don't name things after people. It was a principle we felt we couldn't break and so we lost the donation – but created the library anyway with money from another source.'

'I see. Can I ask you another question?'

'Please do.'

'How do you bury your dead in England?'

'We don't have a Tower of Silence here unfortunately.'

'Well, we don't have vultures here either.'

'You don't need vultures – you have crows. But in 1861 we bought a burial plot in Brookwood – it's near Woking – where we have either cremation or interment available, according to wishes. Jal and Bapsy Pavry had hollow graves at Brookwood, in case they died in England. They didn't need them in the end, but we put inscriptions on them anyway.'

'What do the inscriptions say?'

'Oh nothing. Very simple.'

'But can you tell me what?'

'Yes, of course. Just so-and-so, the name – with the dates.'

POSTSCRIPT

The problem of Bapsy's Will was resolved when Winchester City Council at long last refurbished a reception room in the Guildhall and named it after her. It was opened in June 2009 and is dominated by Frank Salisbury's 'big gaudy' portrait. And Keith McVeigh tells me that the Augustus John portrait of Bapsy, which hung in the Royal Academy, was sold at Christie's in 2000 for £7,637, a little over half its estimate.

CHAPTER THREE

Waiting for Maruma

Scotland is not a place I'd normally wish to visit, but Luca was persuasive. 'I want you to do the story,' he said. It was sunny and surprisingly warm in the late summer of 1995 when he flew to London from Zurich. We met at King's Cross Station, 11.30 am on a Friday, and took the express up to Edinburgh. I still had my doubts and felt displaced; I'd done the Scottish capital some years before and had no reason to hang about there. Neither fortunately did Luca who found our connection and chivvied me on to the Highland railway which transported us before sundown to Mallaig on Scotland's west coast.

We spent the night in a B&B with pink plastic curtains and the following morning boarded a ferry to the Hebrides. This was more like it. I remember as a young boy, three or four years old – this is one of my earliest memories from when my family lived in Harrow – being deeply affected by the song 'The Skye Boat Song'. Not that I knew where Skye was, but the song was a popular radio request and something sweetly strange and yearning touched me even at that age, not only in the beauty of the tune but also through the sound effects of waves and seagulls on the recording. Is this early evidence of a vagabond soul? And now fifty years later the Hebrides were happening to me for the very first time. The interpenetration of sea, sky and land, in which no one element dominated the others or was indeed readily discernible from them, struck an exalted note which lifted our spirits. Well, Luca's didn't need lifting but mine did (it had been a rotten year).

But we were sailing not to Skye but to its small, secretive neighbour, the Isle of Eigg. At our advance it rose from the sea like a fortress of pewter and was distinguished by a dramatic natural feature at its centre, a tower of rock, which at our present distance resembled a shark's fin, giving the prospect an air of menace out of Rider Haggard or Steven Spielberg. On deck I buttoned up my Levi's jacket and was grateful for its quilted lining because there was a chilly edge to the wind. The ferry bumped and foamed through fluttering waters and as it came closer, Eigg's forbidding outline inflated into three dimensions. Detail emerged in bright colours – green, purple, brown, splashes of red and white – and Luca started to bob about with his camera. The island is only twenty-four square miles in extent but has a great variety of landscape due to the distortions brought about by the cooling and erosion of volcanic rock. Among its craggy elevations, dominated always by that massive, threatening plug of stone, we would discover flowery meadows, pocket woods and lakes, and little lush valleys. I'd never seen anything like it. Joseph Brodsky, in his poem *Odysseus to Telemachus*, claims that to a wanderer, all islands look more or less the same. But this is untrue. A wanderer is not a blind man and every island has its particulars. At first glance it was already clear why an artist had bought this one.

Nothing else was clear about that arrangement. Who was this artist from somewhere in Germany who had paid four million marks to become the new Laird of Eigg? Why did he call himself Maruma when his real name, according to newspaper clippings, was Marlin Eckhard? If that *was* his real name. Maybe it was Martin or Merlin or Mertin. These things do get garbled. And where had the money come from and what were Marlin's plans? The sixty-five or so inhabitants of the island were especially keen to have a response to the last question, since their personal futures depended on it: they were his tenants. Reportedly he had purchased the island – and them – after flying over it in a helicopter, a case of love at first sight. Whereupon Maruma came down to earth and introduced himself and his girlfriend to the locals and conducted himself, apparently, in a charming manner, before getting back into the helicopter, rising into the air, and vanishing over the horizon. Since when – nothing. The islanders had heard and seen absolutely nothing more. Total silence. Utter paralysis. On the other hand the previous laird had been hated. His name was Keith Schellenberg, an Englishman of Liechtenstein descent, and his period of sway had made the islanders welcome any change of ownership whatsoever. They were trying hard to be optimistic.

According to the press reports, Maruma described himself as an artist of fire energy. Well – perhaps he was a Zoroastrian. It would be a good thing if he were, since the Parsis, as we know, are an enterprising bunch. But somehow I doubted he would be. The man operated from an establishment called the Maruma Centre in Stuttgart. I have a number of friends dotted about Germany. None of them knew anything about a Maruma Centre. One tried to contact it and discovered that the Centre was not open to the public. Maruma himself, until the Eigg purchase, was unknown in the art world, and the purchase of Eigg had been his only notable act to date – but was it art? When in doubt, call it an installation. Or a performance. The original and perhaps dangerous aspect of this installation was that it was inhabited by real people of non-submissive character who might well have performance ideas of their own.

It was Luca who first heard about the purchase. I'd met Luca through the editor of *Tages-Anzeiger* who told me to root him out in the East End of London where Luca was living on a photography scholarship. He wore spectacles with heavy frames like Peter Sellers's and I took to him immediately when he said he was learning English from *Blackadder* on television (he was fluent in a couple of months but would sometimes address others as 'My liege'). He told me that the Swiss had loads of scholarships – and that I too could probably get one if I put in the right proposal. His financing was always very glossy, rather mysterious, and quite plentiful. He also asked me if I'd try to get Maruma on the phone and chat him up for a rendezvous on his island.

So I'd rung the Maruma Centre in Stuttgart. Every day Maruma was not there, and I never in fact worked out who was there. Or Maruma was in a meeting. Or Maruma was abroad. Or he couldn't be disturbed – meditating on fire presumably, or even in front of a fire (which is something I very much like doing myself). Then one day the girl said 'Who's calling?' and I, yet again, said who I was, and to my astonishment she said 'Hold on a second' and transferred the call.

'Oh…this is a surprise.' I was wrong-footed and my thoughts were elsewhere.

'Yes.'

'Is that Maruma?'

'Yes.'

'Ah – so – right – well, can you tell me what the Maruma Centre is?'

'It is the place where we are.'

'And your art. Can you tell me about your art?'

'My art?'

'Yes.'

'It is better not on the telephone.'

'What is this fire energy you talk of?'

'You don't know what fire is?'

'Well, can you mail me something about your art?'

'What sort of thing?'

'Some printed stuff perhaps. I haven't the faintest idea what you do.'

'There is no mystery.'

'Oh good. Do you set things on fire?'

'Perhaps there is a mystery. It is better you visit us on Eigg and we discuss it face to face. I am fed up with journalists writing stupid things.'

'I'm a writer. I write books.'

'That is better. Maybe we could write a book about Eigg. Something together. Something poetic.'

Maruma's tone wasn't in the least unfriendly and there was a touch of sadness in his voice which was very appealing. I liked him immediately and cast one eye at the photo of him cut from a German newspaper: chubby gentle face with untidy black hair hanging in long swatches from beneath a black beret worn on one side, and a fluffy black jumper of indecipherable design. Only German artists ever look like this. Which is proof – of sorts – that something was authentic somewhere.

'I could visit you in Stuttgart,' I said, 'but I don't want to.'

'No – I understand – you understand – the fire energy is on Eigg,' he replied.

I was thankful for that. Looking for fire energy in Stuttgart was probably doomed to failure. 'When are you next going to Eigg?'

'I think soon,' he replied.

'Soon? Seriously soon?'

'Yes. We have plans to go there maybe end of the month. Or beginning next month.'

'So we could meet there?'

'Of course.'

He did sound genuine. Therefore Luca and I, on the strength of this, had decided to travel up to Eigg, find somewhere to stay, tuck ourselves in, and wait for him to arrive.

And wait we certainly did.

The island's only hostelry was at Kildonan, a farm belonging to a family called the Carrs. It has a fine stone house facing the broad channel which separates Eigg from the mainland, and entry to it is reached along a gulley filled with ferns and rowan trees. In England the rowan is considered a protection against witchcraft – up here, I'm not so sure. But laden with orange berries at this time of year, the rowans warmed us as we approached Kildonan's front door.

Luca and I spent the first couple of days exploring the island by mountain-bike and eating Mrs Carr's delicious dinners. There were two churches to be visited, one Protestant and the other Catholic, and people – if they went to church at all – usually went to both. There was in addition a grey corrugated iron hut which served the community as a shop and a post-office. It was open on most days and Luca told me that when he first went to the post office he found two women in there, drunk on the floor gurgling like babies. Drinking is the most visible of the island's recreations. Outside the post office a giant litter bin made from wire was piled to the brim and overflowing around its base with the empty scarlet tins of McEwen's Export Beer. The bin stood out like a sentinel among the greens and browns of its setting. But empty scarlet beer tins and empty whisky bottles might be encountered anywhere – in caves, in fields, in the churchyards. Quite a popular idea was to place an empty whisky bottle defiantly upright on an exposed rock.

There was generally a fair number of things lying about. One field in particular had become a cemetery for rusting artefacts. Abandoned cars, ploughs and tractors, ovens and fridges were cast about on the turf as though objects in a sculpture park, and through them a herd of rusty brown cows would usually be shuffling and grazing. Perhaps the sculptor Anthony Gormley had contrived it, since he specialises in violating wild empty spaces. On enquiry however we learned that the islanders had often requested help in carting this stuff away, but the local authority always said that without a deep-water pier it would be too expensive a task. The construction of a deep-water pier had been under discussion for more than thirty years. When more urgent conversation slackened on Eigg, this topic was a regular stand-by.

Of Eigg's seven thousand farmed acres, about half belonged to the Laird's farm; another two thousand acres, mostly sheep and cattle, were managed by the Carrs of Kildonan; the remainder belonged to various crofters centred on the straggling village of Cleadale which hunkers beneath a spectacular ridge of rock several miles long. The first sight of Cleadale reminded me of the opening of Peake's *Titus Groan* wherein is described the village beneath the huge walls of Gormenghast Castle, its mean dwellings granted, by ancient law, a 'chill intimacy with the stronghold that loomed above them'. Peake goes on to describe the black tower at the centre of the castle 'which arose like a mutilated finger from among the fists of knuckled masonry and pointed blasphemously at heaven,' and one cannot help being reminded of the natural rock tower which does something very like that at the centre of Eigg.

The Cleadale crofters did have security according to ancient rights. But the Carrs perversely did not. Their farm was subject to a different, murkier arrangement. Such are the knotted anomalies of old, lonely places. And what of Maruma who had stumbled into this faraway bog of hope and tradition? Rumours had started to hot up. The end of the month was in sight and Maruma the Deliverer was said to be arriving at the week-end. That evening at Kildonan I asked Colin Carr if he'd heard anything more specific concerning the Laird's visit. He was nervous and said he'd heard nothing. Dinner was quiet – there was one other couple staying and they were tired from a day's hike-about.

After dinner Luca and I sat either side of the dying fire in the sitting-room, sinking into cushioned easy chairs, and we gradually finished the remains of the claret. The rest of the house fell silent. Strong winds moaned beyond the walls, and the cold and sullen seas heaved blackly all round the island. For the first time we felt far away, on this exposed, northern tip of Europe. Luca lit another cigarette and said 'I've had an offer of a job in Venice after this. Would you like to come too?'

'Thanks. But I don't think I would.'

'You don't want to go to Venice?'

'No, I don't.'

'Did you have a bad experience there?'

'No, I've never been to Venice. There's lots of places I don't want to visit and Venice is one of them.'

'Oooo – why not?'

Luca was amazed. His glass had come to a halt in mid-air. People say 'You must go to Venice, you'll love it', but they said the same about that other vision on water, New York, and when I did go to New York I found what struck me as giant sculpture, curiously inert. Not that I have a problem with cities-and-water per se. Those other water-mounted extravaganzas, Istanbul and St Petersburg, have meant much to me in the past, but they were cities animated by the warmth of poverty. Are rich cities necessarily cold to the heart? Venice, of velvet and marble, was always a rich town and is now immobilised beneath cling-film: the most expensive, most useless city in Italy. Simply to breathe its air is to drain one's credit card.

Of course Venice circulates in the bloodstream of world culture. It is international, that is to say nowhere, and everyone has a chip of it in their brain. It is city as exhibit, as inauthentic experience. Do you think the search for authentic experience is doomed in our modern world? I don't. But one must be mindful of having everything wrapped up for you by others. When did you last buy vegetables to which the earth still clung? Exactly. This is Venice:

vegetables rinsed and trimmed in a see-through container. You see, we are afraid of authenticity – and yet we hunger for it. We are afraid of it because it involves loss of control. We hunger for it because we have so little, in the developed world at least. We have civility instead of authenticity, because lots of authenticity means a life close to violence. I'm looking forward to ocean-wonder Rio de Janeiro, mugging capital of the world, which illustrates the surprising truth that authenticity is the crucible of dreams.

When did Venice stop being real? And therefore, paradoxically, lose its magic? After John Addington Symonds and Baron Corvo? It began earlier, not long after the death of Byron I guess. In 1851 John Ruskin, outraged, reported that the arcades of the Doge's palace were in use by tourists as a latrine; but the city had already been ruined for him by the arrival of the railway several years before. Mind you, travelling writers are always like this. I loved Penang before the airport was built. Pre-airport Penang will always remain my dream of the Orient; and its capital, Georgetown, my ideal of a maritime oriental town: all the charms of the East in a pocket edition (as I wrote to my friend Justin Wintle – who preserved the postcard!). On reflection I'd say that Venice experienced the kiss of death the day Wagner stepped into the foyer of the Danieli.

Luca laughed and clapped his hands. 'More wine, vicar?' he asked – *Blackadder* again. 'I don't like Wagner either.'

I said that I didn't mind Wagner and that Wagner wasn't exactly the point. Vampirism was the point; Wagner's vampirism on Venice; which Wagner later emphasised by travelling there to die, confirming that this was no longer a city but a stage-set available for the greatest death-scene of his career. The Wagners had rented fifteen rooms in the gloomy and sumptuous Palazzo Vendramin where the composer would sit in the windows of the salone overlooking the Grand Canal, illuminated by the winter sun and dressed for death in a black jacket of quilted satin. As his heart gave out, Wagner struck extravagant, almost meaningless attitudes, declaring for example that the best which could happen to anyone in life was to be exiled to Ceylon. The arrival of Liszt at the palazzo did not thin the atmosphere. In Max Ophüls's film *Lola Montès*, Lola says to Liszt that for her life is *movement*, but it was even truer of Liszt than of his mistress. He was probably the most peripatetic man of his time. He was also Wagner's father-in-law and only challenger; indeed musically he had moved way beyond Wagner, who found Liszt's spare late style incomprehensible and dissonant. In these last compositions of Liszt the Modern Movement has already arrived, while Wagner at the end had become obsessed with a popular song, *Harlequin, thou must perish...*

Luca had got me going and, if I may, I'd like to develop the theme here with a consideration of what magic might be. I would assert that the essence of magic is that it not be commonplace. Yes – conformism and magic are enemies. Magic demands the shock of the unexpected and the vibration of difference, not the comfort of sameness. Magic can be upsetting, is inconvenient, marks you. For those who don't want that, there's glamour. Paris – Monte Carlo – Hollywood – New York – Venice – these places have glamour before you go and after you come back, but strange to say, they usually don't have it while you are actually there – this is because when you're there you are too busy trying to photograph your experience with your mind. Quite a few places have both glamour and magic – Rome is a clear example – and they are indeed wonderful places to visit, but the number of such places is in rapid decline and most of them these days are in South America, the unmined continent.

They say Venice is beautiful. In my imagination it is spectacular, but I suspect that if I went, I'd find not spectacle but a toy. It would look smaller, more trite than in my imagination, the way film stars do when you chance upon them in a fashionable restaurant. Venice lacks mystery because it lacks ambivalence. Almost everyone comes away disappointed in some respect. You get less than you pay for.

Though once famously well-organised in the arts of licentiousness, Venice is no longer erotic. It is a desexed city. In Venice you will never meet anyone. The nearest you may come to it is, well, occasionally people will see themselves reflected in other people's eyes. So I guess once in a while people might imagine they've had sex in Venice, or at least been smitten by someone drifting down a street, but it is only imaginary. Too much imagination, too little giving. I expect no one gives in Venice.

The crucial factor in all adventures is *the gift*. Something coming at you unannounced, unscheduled, free of charge, impossible to refuse. It is important to remember this. And it could no more happen in Venice than it could in, say, Saint Tropez. Should you by any chance imagine that you have met someone in Venice, do take them away, out of town, anywhere, but take them away quickly.

Because only then will you be able to see them. If you remain in Venice, you will never see them. Venice is so jealous of lovers. Having rendered them coy, it erases them with ridicule.

Yes, Venice has been too much adored, and its only chance was to become decadent, but mass tourism put a stop to that. The Victorians could enjoy Venice because it was a city dying, a city enacting the myth of Atlantis before their very eyes. Then something terrible happened. A sort of cryonic engineering came along and said 'Thou shalt not die. Thou shalt exist as a cripple for ever.' The moment of psychic extinction, when its last nerve-endings briefly flashed before going out altogether, was – one might as well pin it on this – the funeral of Diaghilev. He died from surfeit at the beach hotel on the Lido, having beforehand sent a telegram to Coco Chanel and Misia Sert who were cruising on the Duke of Westminster's yacht in the Adriatic – 'Am sick: come quickly!' The burial took place on the island of San Michele. Four mourners were present (some accounts add a fifth, a cousin). In addition to the two women there was the most recent ex-lover, Serge Lifar (lately ousted in Diaghilev's heart by a teenage Russian pianist) and Diaghilev's assistant, Boris Kochno – also an ex. Lifar and Kochno had fought from opposite sides of the deathbed while the maestro, still mid-departure, periodically raised his weary eyes to the ceiling. Four mourners merely, at the great Diaghilev's funeral in Venice on a hot August day in 1929. That was when the Venice story ended. The city has been trying to drown itself ever since. But people in dark suits and diamonds and silk and richly crowned or implanted teeth, gathering in passionately concerned groups all over the planet, refuse to let it happen. So the bloated, floating hag known as *la serenissima* is kept on a life-support system of paralysed myth and hard cash. Venice isn't a city, it's a charity. But of course, one couldn't let it sink without a fight because it would become the brazen herald of that eco-disaster waiting to engulf us all.

Cheated of its own grand demise, Venice stares at you like an idiot. Maybe once not so long ago it had the good taste to be embarrassed by being an object of such pity. Now it takes everything it can get. It lacks the profundity of death, because only the living can die. Even *Death in Venice* is not death in Venice but Mann, Mahler, Vienna. Vienna once ruled Venice and the Emperor of Austria-Hungary, who liked double-barrelled titles, was once the King of Lombardy-Venetia.

In my thoughts Venice keeps transmogrifying into Vienna as though one instinctively passes from the sterile to the fertile, because one searches vainly the last hundred years for a significant Venetian-born artist or writer – more Italian poets have been born in Egypt (Marinetti, Ungaretti). Nor in the same period has Venice served foreign poets very well. Rilke's 'Late Autumn in Venice' is, to put it mildly, uninspired. He should have tried something like 'Late Autumn in Oslo'. Oslo is not the most happening town but 'Late Autumn in Oslo' sounds as though it would be a far more interesting poem. It's the mental laziness of using Venice which is the turn-off. Italians themselves never find any fascination there and they avoid it. Venice is an elision of 'very nice', a place for Sunday painters and retirement holidays. I'm not attacking retired people if that's where they want to go. Venice itself is retired. But once a year it tries to pass itself off as youthful. It has a carnival, a masquerade for people who must book via the internet the limited number of places available; and as for Venice's nightclubs, my Italian friends tell me they are the worst in Italy. Which is a melancholy fact for this erstwhile city of revelry and freedom. Travellers travel in search of freedom and therefore should avoid Venice which is under permanent occupation and where their minds will be incarcerated in cliché.

Unable to drown itself, Venice lacks even the power to drown others. The great drownees, Shelley and Le Corbusier for example, gulped their last elsewhere. Although people do not drown in Venice, they do get submerged, trapped in an aqua fantasy between life and death, and instead of expiring they go on and on and on about it in their semi-sozzled purgatory, about this or that church, this or that palace, this or that restaurant. But nobody has an adventure in Venice, as nobody has an adventure in Disneyland or Harrod's. Adventure has been edited out of the programme because adventure is commercially unreliable. And Venice's allure becomes a Pavlovian reflex like that of the Pyramids of Giza or the Taj Mahal or Las Vegas. How very different – indeed the recollection of it makes me shudder still – was my encounter with the great pyramids of Teotihuacan outside Mexico City where atop the Pyramid of the Moon I discovered that the dipping and rising wind howls faintly but unceasingly for murder, with a nagging insistence which interferes with the rhythm of one's heart.

Luca drew my attention to the winds outside our very window, louder, more full-bodied than those in

Mexico, yet ablast with a comparable venom, and said that some places were necessarily not about exposure but about shelter, that Venice was about being sheltered by civilisation, at which I gave ground and granted him a point. He went on 'So is there absolutely nothing you would enjoy in Venice?'

All right – what I'd like, perhaps, is to be smuggled one night across the lagoon in a closed gondola, guided by a single lamp and manoeuvred through side channels to the obscure entrance of the Palazzo Albrizzi. Rising from the canal, coiled in strands of mist, we climb green and slippery steps to find ourselves in a vaulted chamber. Shadows flicker everywhere from the disturbed water. Ahead, a monumental staircase of mottled marble draws us up – the building is uninhabited – of course it is – and silent too, apart from the slurping echoes of the canal. We cross the upper landing with a shiver and find our way by stealth to the ballroom where we should sit awhile and contemplate the wonder of this space whose ceiling of curtained plasterwork – oh, the incomparable plasticity of the Italians - is held aloft in rouches by flying cherubs, a ceiling which for once, mercifully, is unpainted. The Italians loved to paint their rooms and they have the finest painted rooms in the world – but sometimes, Orlando, desist! Candlelight is all this room requires for perfection and when so lit at night the walls and ceiling appear to be alive with swarms of pale rats. The Palazzo Albrizzi is one of those rarities, a Venetian residence with a garden, and through the windows, ajar, come the scents of orange blossom and jasmine on a warm night...

I can't stand being herded. It's one of my problems in

life. And I know there is rarely any other way to explore Venice than as one of the herd. I wish I could be a herd member. I long for it, to be one of the crowd. I can understand why people enjoy war, as a way of joining up with the herd. But the days when I'd relish being in the thick of it at some pop festival for example, those days have passed – now I'd get claustrophobia. I don't think Venice is the place to try and overcome my anti-herd instinct because there is too much coming at you at the art level which makes for extra sensitivity anyway. Venice's ornate bulbousness, arising from its own reflection, has become Narcissus crushed by the charging hooves of bison.

Am I being cruel to poor, drunken Venice? Like a thwarted lover perhaps. My inability to have Venice for myself, the necessity of sharing it, means that I hate it and reject it. I don't want something that's been so handed around; don't want to discharge where all the rest have discharged. And is it the romantic in me who can yearn only for the unattainable? I have always yearned for Venice's great antecedent, Tenochtitlan, capital of the blood-soaked, heart-ripping Aztecs, perhaps the greatest lacustrine city in the world. At the time of the Cortés conquest, it was larger than any city in Europe – so they say.

The nearest I have come to a genuine experience of Venice is reading Brodsky's prose work *Watermark*. He fell in love with Venice because for him it was the inauthentic, therefore containable and bearable version of his seething, super-charged home town of St Petersburg. Everyone, unless he's mindless, has a complex relationship with his place of origin and, given that Russian history is probably the most terrifying of all histories, perhaps this is truest of Russians. St Petersburg has more bridges than Venice but is as blood-soaked as Tenochtitlan. The expatriate option – or exile, its involuntary counterpart – can solve many problems in the short term, and remember – our lives are short. For Brodsky, having been rejected by St Petersburg, Venice becomes paramour on the rebound, because Venice never refuses an advance, is open to all. Yet *Watermark* is a thin book, a polished letter to a courtesan. Even for Brodsky, Venice is not a place where anything much is born and he confesses that he would never go there in summer-time, not even at the point of a gun. I was going to meet Brodsky in New York once, but he had a stroke, or a heart attack, one of those ailments, and the meeting was postponed until he got better – but he didn't get better and is buried in the same cemetery as Diaghilev. Shame. I could have put to him these doubts about Venice. I have often mentioned them to others, a few of whom agree with me but most do not and go into a kind of promo-paroxysm as though it's essential that I be converted to the faith. Barbara Cartland had no doubts. 'Been dozens of times!' she swooped. 'Adore it, written heaps about it, got loads of friends there – there's a duke who gave me a party in his palace all lit up with candles, as it would've been in the eighteenth century. Venice doesn't change which is good because every other place is always changing.'

And we haven't yet mentioned the absence of cars. But I'm not convinced. Natale Maganuco, a Sicilian, said to me 'The feeling I have is that Venice...emotionally it is lost. It has been wonderful but is now something unreal. Even the Venetians are something unreal.' In fact do Venetians exist any more than do Ruritanians? One suspects not, and outsiders pour in to view the amazingly decked-out corpse of a unique urbanism. Oh, forgive me if I've gone on too long, but the true horror of Venice is that its fate, in a world of too many people, could well be the fate of all beautiful places: the fenced-off national park as much as the railed-off cameo township, trampled because protected, polluted because isolated, degraded because valued. Eventually the only beautiful places will be inside us. What a revolting thought.

•

The night winds dropped, the following day was again sunny, and Eigg glowed with warmth. The principal house of the island is called the Lodge and is the seat of the Laird. I found it down a winding lane among sheltered woods. The tranquillity was deep and birdsong enhanced it. Even the sea which is everywhere at hand on Eigg could not be heard here. Propping my bike against mildewed gates, and trusting that the weight of the machine would not bring to ground the tenuous fretwork of wood, I ventured up the drive. The site was deserted. Rhododendrons and blue & white hydrangeas, running continuously along either side, were interrupted every so often by outrageous palm trees. At the top of a low rise, and at a considered angle, a villa appeared in a glade. It had a steeply pitched roof and was flanked by matching pavilions. To the left was a derelict tennis court, to the right an orchard thoroughly overgrown.

I stood for some time staring at the broken red clay of the tennis court and I recalled another lodge, of exactly the same reddish colour as the court, which I'd visited many

years before with Sarah Moffett in New Delhi, the Viceregal Lodge of the Viceroys of India. There is endless debate
about the correct term for this Versailles of British India.
Someone told us it should be called 'Viceregal Lodge'
without the definite article. Someone else said no, it should
be called 'Viceroy's House' because 'Viceregal Lodge' was
the place up at Simla – which does make more sense. And
I recalled those wartime invitations to Bapsy Pavry which
I'd seen in Winchester – they'd been sent from 'The Viceroy's House', but of course war changes things, even little
things like that. What I remember most poignantly from
that morning in 1975 when Sarah and I had tea with the
President of India, in what was no longer called Viceroy's
anything but 'the Raj Bhavan,' was that she and I broke
away from the main party, left them to their porcelain cups
and pink and lemon iced cakes, in order to explore the gardens. Sadly these were neglected. The peacocks had vanished, the ornamental fountains and tanks were dry. And
we came to a tennis court similarly derelict, and we sat
beside it with the long grass round our legs until I detected
a lump beneath my foot, and rummaging in the tangled
undergrowth I extracted an ancient blackened tennis ball
which had obviously been struck and forgotten many years
before by a departing British Raj player. I wish now I'd
kept it as a souvenir, that very last viceregal tennis ball, but
instead I flung it the length of an unkempt terrace where it
disappeared once again into the maw of history.

A rasping arpeggio of bird noise recalled me from the
Indian Empire to the Lodge at Eigg where my two feet
were firmly anchored to the earth. The bird spoke again – a
magpie – that unpleasant rattling call. In front of the house

a semi-circle of red fuchsia bushes enclosed the Laird's lawn. Those fuchsias were great travellers too, since the plants are native to South America. I was surely in the most sheltered spot on the island, thickly wooded in every direction, enjoying the best of Eigg's microclimate borne up by the warm waters of the Gulf Stream. The atmosphere around the house was charged with an improbable *douceur*. It was another world really, a surreal outpost of Thames Valley affluence transported across wild Celtic seas to arrive intact at this protected place.

Personally I've never liked fuchsias and would rip them out if the property were mine. Coming closer, I peer in through the windows. Bare floorboards. A small drawing-room with art deco detail and some garden furniture stacked in it, otherwise no furnishing at all. The house was empty, with the magnetic pull of all empty houses. From its arcaded porch I heard the tinkle of a falling stream. The air was clammy and still. Yes, the Lodge too was waiting – but somehow not for Maruma.

That evening a little enquiry back at Kildonan was productive. The villa had been put up in the nineteen-twenties by Sir Walter Runciman, later Baron Runciman, when he was the Laird of Eigg. Subsequently it was inherited, along with the rest of the island, by his two sons. One of them was the Byzantinist Steven Runciman and I thought I'd give him a ring at his house on the mainland at Lockerbie – I'd had some doings with him years before and retained the number. He was ninety-two years old when we spoke on this occasion but he recalled Eigg with instant affection. I wondered how long the island had been in his family and asked 'Did your father inherit it too?'

'No, he didn't. But he'd fallen in love with it and it was for sale for practically nothing and he was tempted.'

'And how often did you go there?'

'I went for about three months a year–for forty years. In August my brother always had it. We went for New Year to celebrate with the tenants, and we gave a children's party every year, so I knew all the islanders. There were no real difficulties. Now and again they tried to pull a fast one, but we made light of it and all got on rather well.'

'The climate is so mild.'

'Yes, it could be wet and windy but there was seldom any frost. I often went to write, taking a suitcase of books and groceries. A very good place for work and there were always mackerel and lobsters to eat. May, June was my favourite time. But there was often very good weather in December.'

'Were you ever bored there?'

'No. Why should I have been?'

'I adore the Lodge.'

'I'm glad you like that. Our idea was more a Mediterranean villa. We planted the palms. We didn't want awful imitation Scots baronial. And it was a very easy house to run.'

'When did you sell up?'

'1966. The place is not very suitable as you get older,' he explained, 'because it's not very easy to get to. Our excellent factor had to retire and the thought of finding a new one, with a wife who wouldn't mind living there in isolation, was rather daunting. I have the happiest memories of the island and, I must say, it's distressing what's happened since. Very few of our tenants are left but I feel almost disloyal in allowing the place to get into disreputable hands. We sold to a Welsh farmer, Mr Evans, who thought it would be profitable as a farm. He sold it on at a great profit, but apologised to us for doing so. He said that the profit only realised what he had lost over the period. We ran the farm so that we didn't lose much. But one always lost something. Eigg is an expensive pastime, you know. It was then taken over by a chancer who wanted to establish it as a school for deficient boys who would do all the work for nothing and he would be paid for taking them on, but I don't think he could get a license from the county council.'

'What about Keith Schellenberg?'

'I rather like him but he's a mixed-up kid.'

'And now Maruma.'

'Don't know him but he'll be good only if he's prepared to spend money on it.'

'And have you been back since you sold?'

He made a short noise, somewhere between a sigh and a laugh. 'No...I don't believe in going back to places you've loved, to places where you've been very happy. I think it's always a mistake to do that.'

Heavy clouds exploded across the blue sky bringing wind and rain. We watched television, read books and magazines, and one evening went for dinner at the house of Mrs Carr's sister in Cleadale. When we arrived she was straining simmered blackberries through a cloth. A dark blood-coloured liquid spilled over the edge of the bowl to yelps of pleasure from her children. Though not well-off in money terms, people can live wonderful lives here if they don't hanker for the amenities of a conurbation. Mrs Carr's sister said 'We heard that Maruma is sending £30,000 for urgent repairs.'

One of the crofters, Micky, decided to throw a party in his kitchen. We all jammed in there on the cement floor under a bright light, hedged around by stacks of beer, whisky and cigarettes. Rock music, tinny and very loud, squirted from the radio/cassette player. I was reminded of Russia. Because of the squeeze, you couldn't really see people's bodies. The party was all heads and smoke and noise. Like most of the crofters, Micky was an incomer, not born on Eigg. In fact the crofters came more out of hippiedom than out of farming. An intense, Pre-Raphaelite girl asked 'Is there any truth in the rumour that Maruma is penniless?' Another rumour too was going round, that the successful businessman Richard Branson had tried to buy the island but Maruma got in first. An ample, kindly woman materialised out of the fug and introduced herself as Maggie. With the rock-music noise sizzling across her speech I was barely able to determine that she came from Bolton in Lancashire and was secretary of the Eigg Community Association. She said that Maruma's master plan – his what? – *master plan*! for the island had just arrived in the post – had what? – *just arrived in the post and I've pinned it up in my cottage*. Would we like to go over and look at it?

The following afternoon, rather thick in the head, we did. It was cosy by her fire with mugs of tea. A Pan-like boy from Huddersfield slouched and smiled in a chair. He didn't say much. He ran a hand every so often through his tousled curls and years afterwards, to my surprise, I found myself using him in a novel. Craft objects were for sale. Maggie's forte was knitted winter socks of an eskimo kind and I bought several pairs as presents. And there on a sheet pinned up and hanging the height of the room was

Maruma's *Long Term Concept*. It was very long indeed. We carried our mugs closer. He was hoping to change everything. Among the proposed developments were a fast ferry service, holiday cottages, the conversion of the Lodge to an holistic health centre, horse-breeding, fish-farming, removal of rubbish, renovation of buildings, a sports hall, indoor swimming-pool, shopping centre – it took one's breath away and seemed over the top. Maggie pulled a funny face at it and handed me another mug of tea. Warming liquids are the blood of social life up here. The Huddersfield boy was about to say something but stretched his legs out instead and stared at his denim crotch.

I asked Maggie if there were any crofters who weren't hippies and she said 'There's Mr and Mrs McEwen. Theirs is one of only three or four households here who speak Gaelic.'

The McEwens – who are nothing to do with the beer McEwens – lived in an old cottage facing west over the sea. Inside it looked like the nineteen-fifties. Or do I mean the eighteen-fifties? Lawrence McEwen remembered the time of the Runcimans as Eigg's golden age but his account of it differed somewhat from Steven's.

'Lord Runciman got the island very cheaply. The previous owner had been borrowing from him, so Runciman virtually owned the island before he bought it. In those days there was a dairy which produced fresh milk and cheese and butter. Now all we have is this terrible long-life milk. Hate the stuff. And there were jobs for everyone. Lord Runciman employed six rabbit catchers for example. And very good shooting there was. Do you know the Game Law here? You can shoot pheasant if they stray onto your property but you're not allowed to lift them. They all belong to the Laird. To this German feller now.'

'Have Germans ever come here before?' I ask.

'Only dead ones,' says Mr McEwen. 'Washed up on the beach during the war.'

Without looking up from her knitting, Mrs McEwen, bespectacled, a woman dour in the extreme, nods agreement with her husband, as though the ironies of life could go no further. The light coming off the sea is metallic and the waves sound meaty and round, falling on the beaches below. 'We don't count him,' she says after a while. For some reason I know she's referring to the island's ex, Keith Schellenberg.

'And mines too,' says Mr McEwen. 'We used to get explosive mines washed up on the beach.'

'Do you ever go to the city?'

Lawrence McEwen glances at his wife as though I've said something dangerous.

'Occasionally,' she replies, 'but I don't like the sea-crossing.'

'Does the city frighten you?'

She pauses and looks up. 'We take it in our stride,' she says.

Luca took some photographs. Unless it is absolutely unavoidable I never talk to people while they are being photographed because it makes them too self-conscious to give me their attention. But the McEwens took that in their stride too. Photographs, reporters, the press – Eigg doesn't care much about that sort of thing. Water off a duck's back. A sentimental view would be that places like Eigg bring out the genuine in people, for better or worse.

I think it's not that but, you know, living in such close proximity to the attentions of others, you'd be dour too. They drink to shake off, briefly, the chains of never rocking the boat.

That night we discovered that an Italian couple were staying at the farmhouse, academics from Bologna, and Mrs Carr produced a surpassing dinner of smoked fish, roast lamb, and a hot fruit sponge with cream. Italians have a thing about Scotland, perhaps because it is the opposite end of Europe for them, and my first proper tour of Scotland was at the behest of my Sicilian friend Natale: and we discovered on our drive through the Highlands that there were more Italian visitors than any other kind.

Luca was delighted to have the opportunity of speaking his native tongue but they didn't overdo it and I learned that the female academic had been involved with the excavations at Pompeii. I said 'As Venice gradually sinks into inundation, so Pompeii gradually rises from it.' She said the former was happening too fast and the latter not fast enough. I questioned her on the Villa dei Papiri at Herculaneum, with its tantalising promise of lost masterpieces from Classical Literature coming to light, but that wasn't her area and she was unable to tell me how affairs went on there. But she had done some work in connection with the digitalisation of the sites, the provisional results of which I'd already seen at an exhibition which came to London three years previously. Next day the weather was bad and the Italians lent me a book on Pompeii which they had with them. It was in Italian, which I can't properly read, but it beguiled an hour or so on the bed as the rain smacked against the windows.

Naturally the photographs occupied me more than the text and I experienced an intense recollection of my first visit to Pompeii which was one Italian springtime while staying in Ravello. I wrote of it in *To Noto* and shan't repeat that here but I saw, as I flicked shiny pages, that this Italian book quoted several letters from English travellers to Pompeii. One was from Roger Fry to his mother. I've since tracked down the original English. He was visiting Pompeii in the spring of 1891, and wrote from the Hotel Victoria at Cava dei Tirreni:

It is far more complete than I had expected, some of the buildings even having the roof left. The baths are especially delightful; the niches for putting one's clothes in, the braziers for heating the rooms, everything quite complete. But the whole effect is quite wonderful of going from street to street and from one private house to another just as though one was in a modern town with free access to all the houses. They are very similar and one ground plan would serve for nearly all but of course there are slight modifications and the colouring is very varied. The decorations are extremely delicate and beautiful and in most of the rooms it is so perfect that one can get a good idea of what they looked like. Everything is absurdly small, the shops being often only about 8 feet square and the streets, even the broadest, only about as wide as Bank Place...I am writing this in a room with a large fire and listening to a young lady singing Schubert, so that one can hardly complain of being unhomely...

Pompeii can be a very hot place to explore, even in spring. The dark volcanic rock holds the heat and the site is treeless and without other shade. Few of the buildings are roofed, although there have been discussions concerning the legitimacy of a roofing programme. I'm against it in theory, because it would turn the place into a mock-up, but for it in practice. In the event, sweating profusely, I was moved to tears by the experience because unlike most ruins, where the religious or warlike element is paramount, at Pompeii it is the human factor which is so strong. The Forum was smaller than the market square at Wantage! This humanity has always been the principal legacy to us from the classical world of Greece and Rome. How close to us it seems, in comparison with the primitive gibberish from elsewhere. And you enter Pompeii by the Nocera road which is lined with funerary monuments, now reborn to remind us once again of the oblivion which awaits us all.

Herculaneum was rediscovered before Pompeii. The official date for the former is 1738. Horace Walpole, on the Grand Tour, was relatively quick off the mark and wrote to his friend Richard West from Naples on June 14th 1740:

One hates writing descriptions that are to be found in every book of travels; but we have seen something to-day that I am sure you never read of, and perhaps never heard of. Have you ever heard of a subterranean town? a whole Roman town, with all its edifices, remaining under ground? Don't fancy the inhabitants buried it there to save it from the Goths: they were buried with it themselves; which is a caution we are not told they ever took. You remember in Titus's time there were several cities destroyed by an eruption of Vesuvius, attended with an earthquake. Well, this was one of them, not very considerable, and then called Herculaneum. Above it has since been built Portici, about three miles from Naples, where the King has a villa. This under-ground city is perhaps one of the noblest curiosities that ever has been discovered. It was found out by chance, about a year and a half ago. They began digging, they found statues; they dug further, they found more. Since that they have made a very considerable progress, and find continually. You may walk the compass of a mile; but by the misfortune of the modern town being overhead, they are obliged to proceed with great caution, lest they destroy both one and t'other. By this occasion the path is very narrow, just wide enough and high enough for one man to walk upright. They have hollowed, as they found it easiest to work, and have carried their streets not exactly where were the ancient ones, but sometimes before houses, sometimes through them. You would imagine that all the fabrics were crushed together; on the contrary, except some columns, they have found all the edifices standing upright in their proper situation. There is one inside of a temple quite perfect, with the middle arch, two columns, and two pilasters. It is built of brick plastered over, and painted with architecture: almost all the insides of the house are in the same manner; and, what is very particular, the general ground of all the painting is red. Besides this temple, they make out very plainly an amphitheatre: the stairs, of white marble, and the seats are very perfect; the inside was painted in the same colour with the private houses, and great part cased with white marble. They have found among other things some fine statues, some human bones, some rice, medals, and a few paintings extremely fine. These latter are preferred to all the ancient paintings that have ever been discovered. We have not seen them yet – as they are kept in the King's apartment, whither all these curiosities are transplanted; and 'tis difficult to see them – but we shall...

There might certainly be collected great light from this reservoir of antiquities, if a man of learning had the inspection of it; if he directed the working, and would make a journal of the discoveries. But I believe there is no judicious choice made of directors. There is nothing of the kind in the known world; a Roman city entire of that age, and that has not been corrupted with modern repairs. Besides scrutinising this very carefully, I should be inclined to search for the remains of the other towns that were partners with this in the general ruin. 'Tis certainly an advantage to the learned world, that this has been laid up so long. Most of the discoveries in Rome were made in a barbarous age, where they only ransacked the ruins in quest of treasure, and had no regard to the form and being of the building; or to any circumstances that might give light into its use and history.

Walpole's inclination was shared by others in the civilised world and Pompeii came to be discovered ten years after Herculaneum, though he never saw it. Venice is the victim of time, but Pompeii and Herculaneum escaped time for nearly two thousand years. History began again for them in the eighteenth century when these discoveries gave impetus to the Age of Enlightenment and to Neoclassicism in the arts. In the second half of the eighteenth-century Pompeiian decoration became all the rage, with its flat imagery and striking colours – black, green, purple, yellow, blue, vermilion – and numerous Pompeiian rooms appeared right across Europe from the Escorial to St Petersburg, more elegant but less mysterious than the originals. This decorative style, mixing architectural elements, grotesqueries and free-standing images set in large panels of coloured wash, injected a quasi-rococo gaiety into Neoclassicism and was fashionable for a long time (the Pompeiian Room at Ickworth was finished in 1879). These simulations have their own integrity; their function was aesthetic rather than antiquarian, and the gaucheness, for example, of Roman painting (so unlike the exquisite realism of Greek and Roman sculpture) was not reproduced.

My second encounter with Pompeii was on a breezy afternoon five years after my actual visit to the site, and it was indoors: the London exhibition to which I've already made reference. I love museums and therefore one of the regrettable cock-ups on my *To Noto* escapade was that I hadn't realised in advance that Pompeii was actually the ghost of a ghost and all its artefacts had been transferred to Naples, to the National Archaeological Museum set up in the old Bourbon cavalry barracks. On my southwards plunge

I was not going to make a U turn and go back to the objects in Naples. But now some of the objects came to me, two hundred of them, in an exhibition called 'Rediscovering Pompeii' which had stopped off at the Accademia Italiana in Rutland Gate, Knightsbridge, on its journey round the world. These days not only people go travelling; treasures do too, cushioned and boxed and insured, curated and chaperoned, heralded by politicians, diplomats and princes. At one time the circus came to town to astound us with its marvels; now it is the travelling art show. This one comprised green glass jugs, bronze lamps, gold bracelets and earrings, cameo brooches, shapely clay pottery, sublime statuary, bowls and flasks, kitchen and medical implements, etc. There was even a pair of dice on display, most magical of objects (and invented by the Hindus incidentally). Why most magical? Because dice liquefy destiny and break the grip of the inevitable; when you gamble you sunder cause and effect.

Objects are vulnerable and require protection. In return they glorify the possessor and are physical evidence of his custodial power. Do the Elgin Marbles look less in the British Museum than they would back on the Parthenon frieze? In fact they look more. More like sculpture, less like adornment, because we have done the Duchamp trick of taking them out of context and putting them in a gallery. Something similar had happened to the objects at the Pompeii exhibition in London, which were mostly not ornaments but functional objects which had been ornamented. When the objects were in context, they probably attained a sort of inertia, edited out of the attention by quotidian familiarity. Did the Dancing Lar (up on toes, bronze, olive-green patina, about twelve inches high) dance better in the old days back in Pompeii? I think not. Objects as beautifully preserved as this appear to exist outside time. Their whole purpose was to triumph over the ephemeral, the circumstantial.

The eruption began on August 24th 79 AD (how do they work out these dates?) and took only two days to bury Pompeii-Herculaneum under fifteen feet of rubble. Talk about fire energy. The suddenness of the event means that for most of their existence these objects have not participated in life. They were instead transported through a conceptual hyperspace of collapsed time directly to us. They are young in the world. They are the flowers of catastrophe. Time has not been able to work its grinding, daily dose upon them.

To view such things after a journey on the London Underground sitting opposite someone who unnerves you, or after a motorway traffic jam which had you juggling radio stations in desperation, is to mediate further their meaning or, let us say, their relevance. Even the most abstract painting or building can reach us only by passing through filters of the personal. A lamp which is used for light, be it ever so beautiful, will—seen day after day at home—be valued in the first place as a light source, while a lamp in a glass case will never be a light source even for a second. It can only be an object of contemplation. And so, because this lamp is also a beautiful object which once had a function, we fall into a mood of nostalgia, the poignant reverie on a way of life which has gone. This is the second method of giving context to an object: through dreaming. The first is through the study of its history.

History is nostalgia with teeth. Nostalgia is one of the most powerful emotions of the civilised man, not so much in its reductive meaning of nostalgia for a golden age which has passed, but nostalgia as an enriching function of the soul, an activation of Platonic ideal states, a spreading of consciousness beyond the present moment. Many otherwise intelligent men forget that consciousness exists in time as well as space. Since material from the future is limited, this activation tends to employ past material which is plentiful, and so the more intensely one lives in the present, the more susceptible one is to nostalgia. This is what we receive from the object as relic. But the object also receives something from us. As a show-business star is rendered more charismatic by the adoration of audiences, so is an object in a museum or exhibition. The more it is venerated the more venerable it becomes.

Objects, like show-business stars, can acquire such a powerful presence in the imagination that an actual physical encounter may be disappointing. As we have remarked, Venice may well have achieved this on a metropolitan scale. A more modest example would be the case of amplified music on a CD which can be played so cleanly and loudly that to hear the same, say, symphony in a concert hall involves a reduction in stimulus. One must adjust, one must retune, to the acoustic performance. Use of the imperative 'must' is intentional because the live encounter is always superior to the simulated one. Why? Because machines are dead and people are alive. The CD performance is exactly repeatable. The live performance is always unique.

Are museum exhibits 'live' or 'simulated'? The marble

table on show at the Accademia exhibition, on griffon supports with outspread wings, is decidedly the *ding an sich*, but not the *ding in situ*. It has been singularised and immobilised, like the symphony on the CD. We are sometimes told these days that objectification is morally wrong. I can't remember why. Something to do with alienation probably. But it can be extremely exciting and rewarding – not only in a museum but also in sex for example. Individuation is the empowerment of the self and this has to be predicated on a degree of reification of the other, as – to reverse the powerflow – an excess of consideration for the other will inevitably require self-abasement. Some might say that this marble table, like the sex object, degenerates into a component of private fantasy, becomes fodder for a predatory will. Who cares when the result is a revelation and brings forth new life?

The exhibition was sponsored by IBM. Which reminds us that objectification can lead to a pulverisation of experience into sense-data so extensive that only another computer can deal with it. A desiccated world, reconstituted mechanically, is a remarkable achievement in itself but when the external world becomes merely fuel for a contrived world, the facts of life by which we live and die may become increasingly unbearable to us. E.M. Forster wrote a disquieting story on this theme, *The Machine Stops*, a long time ago. This becomes the contemporary equivalent of the great nineteenth-century debate: rural Wordsworthian 'let it be natural' versus urban Baudelairean 'let it be artificial'. The former is Darwinian but spiritual; the latter is religious but atheistic. Do you want the epic, pantheistic experience stumbling round Pompeii? Or the lyric, intellectual experience sniffing round glass cases? Let us have both. Our understanding will operate through reciprocity, a concept we cited in the first chapter.

In the human sphere the most obvious reciprocity between the natural and the artificial is in the realm of sex. Pompeii is a very sexy place – gay, straight, everything between and beyond. Its citizens doubtless went through the emotional tangles we all go through and the ancient world has much to say on romantic love as well as on recreational sex. But they did not veil sexuality and are at home with it in a way that the Christian world never is, nor the Muslim or Jewish worlds. Sex in Pompeii was simply everywhere, openly displayed in pictures, household objects, public statues, graffiti, brothels and books, surviving testimony to the ruthlessness of sexual repression by the religions which came after. Though most of the explicit imagery has, for protection and not from censoriousness, been removed to the Naples museum, Pompeian sexuality still hits you with enormous force when you are there, those divine gifts of pleasure and beauty, anguish and excitement in human life which are sex. Something goaty and awe-inspiring trembles in the air and one cannot help feeling that in the arts of congress the Pompeian would find modern man a curiously worried child. Modern European psychology and art has largely been devoted to repairing this rupture from the elemental which was master-minded in private life by the Church and in public life by the industrial revolution.

Sex, so crucial to the experience of Pompeii, was almost completely absent from this London exhibition, as though sex could have no place in the software of information technology. Sex is far too human – the programmer cringes, turns aside to measure the height of a vase in exact centimetres. Among the many oil lamps on display there was none of Pompeii's most popular kind, the phallic type. Indeed there was only one phallus (i.e. the erect penis) to be seen here at all, an elegant stone abstraction which would have been wedged into the wall of a house to discourage malign influences. Of the countless decorative phalli found all over Pompeii and Herculaneum not one made it to Rutland Gate.

The exhibition refused to be sexy. What it wanted to be was pretty – and it succeeded. Though the space was cramped and the objects bundled in, one was arrested by the grace of objects from the ancient world. The head of an athlete, for example, reminded one that such skill collapsed in the Dark Ages and modelling as unsubmissive and fine as this would not resurface until Donatello. So it was an enthralling prettiness, a *Midsummer Night's Dream*, with nothing of the cute about it, more of the macabre, and I employ the word 'pretty' because of the smallness of scale. One is so accustomed in our cities to a setting all out of scale to ourselves that to find oneself in a world where man is the measure is like finding a world in miniature: human scale has come to mean small scale. But our artificial creation, the City, in outgrowing us, has taken on some attributes of Nature. Phrases like 'the asphalt jungle' (W. R. Burnett, 1949) or 'the concrete jungle' (Desmond Morris, 1969) remind us that the dichotomy between the two sensibilities, artificial and natural, has here been resolved in a way that is close to despair. The general view is that modern cityscapes are at their most appealing at night when they appear to melt into the starry cosmos.

The computers at this exhibition were the offspring of the Neapolis Project, a large computer installation by IBM at the archaeological site itself which aims to record every possible piece of information about Pompeii and its treasures, recycling the accumulation into educational games. According to the publicity, 'One insight identifies restaurants in different districts according to price...' Restaurants in 79 AD or restaurants to-day? Couldn't be sure. Another line of research has been to devise precautions against site-vulnerability in case of another volcanic eruption; Pompeii escaped once from the world and they're determined it won't happen again. Each of the exhibition rooms had a number of video screens incorporating the latest touchscreen techniques. This allowed you to enter and explore the programmes by touching different parts of the screen. Some of them didn't work, or perhaps my fingers aren't hot enough. One became lost in a labyrinth of bits. To add insult to injury, the brilliance of the onscreen images drained the real objects of colour and the vivacity of moving images made the static exhibits akin to wallflowers, party poopers refusing to dance. Thus the images became more real, that is, more vital to the senses, than the exhibits themselves. The computers were intended to serve Pompeii but the reverse was happening. Pompeii became the raw material which enabled the computers to dazzle us with their ingenuity.

But the objects had the final say. Their very silence, their merciless motionlessness, was pregnant with tension, a challenge of hauteur thrown back at the process of digitalisation. These objects, wonderful in themselves, were made numinous by their successors in European art.

We can trace the lines of stylistic procreation backwards to these potent originals. All these objects endure beyond the electronic moment and so prevail. It is the video image which rapidly fades out of the memory, whereas the object squats stubbornly in the imagination by virtue of occupying time and space, refusing to be pulverised.

Pompeii and Herculaneum are of course beyond the capacity of any computer and the archaeological site continues its story in the living world. For example the restorers long inserted reinforced concrete into the fabric, but this turned out to be a disaster, expanding in the heat and causing structures to split, and there has been a return to the original materials from which the Roman towns were built. The attempt to find the perfect weed-killer continues in the battle with resurgent verdure – volcanic soil is so maddeningly fertile. Vesuvius was covered in rich vineyards and was known as the Hill of Bacchus. As a reminder of that, as well as of the inhabitants' physical freedom, there were two marble statues in the London show, naked males leaning backwards and flaunting their slack genitals, one a satyr pouring wine, the other a drunken Heracles peeing. Sex? Nah, just a piss-up…

A third of the archaeological site remains to be dug out and every year fresh controversies burst around new discoveries. Endless numbers of penises keep popping up. The region is geologically unstable. An earthquake in 1980 damaged in some way two-thirds of the excavations. And of course Vesuvius, according to the historical record, is long overdue for another eruption. Most exciting of all is the ancient library unearthed at the Villa dei Papiri in Herculaneum. The first Getty Museum at Malibu in

California is a reproduction of this villa but the original is only now being systematically investigated. New techniques in unravelling scrolls sealed by fire may give us lost or hitherto unknown masterpieces from the dawn of civilised humanity. How great a benefit this would be, were it to trigger another Classical renaissance in Europe, allowing us drink anew from the wisdom of the Greeks and the statecraft of the Romans.

But what I loved quite as much as the exhibits from *that* site was their location at this site: a large, gentle, creamy London house. The Accademia Italiana's premises at 24 Rutland Gate were built in 1841 for a man called John Sheepshanks, a bachelor and cloth manufacturer from Leeds who became an art collector. Henry Cole took Turner to the house in 1851 – *The Survey of London* is telling me these things. In 1899 the house was purchased by Baron Frédéric d'Erlanger who enlarged it and refined the interiors in Parisian taste. He was a member of a European banking family, international plutocrats along the lines of the Camondos, Rothschilds, Bischoffsheims and Sassoons. Frédéric's father was German, his mother American, and he was born in Paris, a Proustian figure who became a naturalised British citizen, combining his career as banker with that of composer – several of his operas were performed at Covent Garden, and there was a ballet, *Le cent baisers*, which made it onto record in the early days of HMV. Heedless of the bombs, the Baron died in London in 1943. As for the Accademia Italiana, it has vanished from these premises. Maybe the organisation is defunct or conducts its activities more reclusively elsewhere.

Yesterday I drove to Rutland Gate to look again at

number 24. It was a dispiriting experience. Who owns the house now? Everything delicate or mellow about the place has been eliminated and its soul eviscerated – there's nothing like an excess of barbarian wealth to destroy a building. Where the garden should be, there was a car park with three glossy new motors. The house itself was lit up inside but empty, decorated in a shrill hotel style, sealed by metal grilles. It is both occupied and unoccupied.

•

At Kildonan Farm the rumour-machine is in full swing. While I've been absorbed in the book on Pompeii, Luca has been downstairs gossiping and he comes up to the bedroom, excitedly pulling on a cigarette. 'He's coming to-morrow, we heard Maruma's coming to-morrow!' he informs me.

'When?'

'On the boat.'

'Which boat?'

'There's only one boat. The mid-day boat.'

'I thought there were other boats.'

'No, no, no, there's only one boat…or are there other boats?' Luca looks concerned and dashes off in search of Colin Carr.

That evening we have a dinner of homemade vegetable soup, roast pork, and a blackberry & apple tart with cream. The Carr's son, Donny, waits on us and clears away the table and I ask him if the house is haunted.

He stops, a plate in each hand, and his reddish complexion colours more deeply. 'Yes.'

'Go on...'

'Well...The stair-carpet rolled upstairs.'

'All by itself?'

'Yes. All by itself. And with all the nails taken out and left on the side.'

'What do you mean, left on the side?'

'The carpet nails were left on the stairs but very neatly and the carpet was in a roll at the top. It happened twice.'

Donny is at Gordonstoun. After the age of eleven there is no schooling on the island and all the children have to go to boarding school but the local authority helps with the cost. I wonder if they teach carpet-laying at Gordonstoun.

By the next day the warm weather has returned and the views are exhilarating. Clouds and islands, hills and mountains and water mix up silver and green, blue and purple and gold in combinations which are unpaintable because they are always in slow motion. Seabirds go up and down, up and down on promontories of rock. Everyone troops along in their wellington boots to the jetty to await Maruma and the midday boat, and I am disconcerted to discover that a number of them are walking unsteadily and slurring their words. I am far from being a prude but I don't think our livers were invented for morning booze. I point to a burnt-out vehicle by the jetty. 'That was Shellenberg's,' says one of the drunks.

Keith Schellenberg was an ageing playboy, a vegetarian and a wildlife enthusiast who declared in a benevolent and defiant proclamation that the whole island would from now on be a nature reserve. Benevolent to the wildlife, defiant of local tradition. He forbad shooting and permitted only limited fishing. At the same time he drove a titanic

Rolls Royce backwards and forwards along the island's only road and played 'war games' across the moors and woods, crags and beaches, with other ageing playboys. During one of them the Nazi flag was seen to fly from the Lodge flagpole. Schellenberg behaved coarsely with the tenants and it all came to a head when he attempted to prise the Carr family out of Kildonan. During the subsequent protests his beloved Rolls Royce was captured and set on fire. Schellenberg abandoned Eigg in a fluster, referring to the islanders as 'rotten, dangerous, and totally barmy revolutionaries.'

Maruma resembles Schellenberg to the extent that his association with Eigg is his chief, perhaps his only distinction. Otherwise Maruma is very different. Schellenberg was unavoidable whereas Maruma is undiscoverable. Maruma is a wraith and, judging from the intermittent vibrations he sends out, he is a New Age wraith. He is also very indecisive. He seems to hang around waiting for the energy to be right–which is a mug's game; to sit in a chair waiting for 'energy' sounds like stalling or depression or inner conflict. Therefore he generates waves of doubt in others. Where are his paintings, said to have sold for enormous sums? They have been searched for but not located. What is this art of fire energy he goes on about? One doesn't expect it to compete with Vesuvius but surely it has heat of *some* kind? I'm told he's a chain-smoker–would that be it? And is there any money? His ex-wife, a woman called Renate, told a reporter that Maruma is not rich in his own right and does not come from a rich family. The Eigg purchase appears to have been funded by a loan of £1.6 million from what one British newspaper has identified as the Volksbank Workers Banking Co-op. Now, they say, problems have arisen over this loan. Where will the additional millions required for investment be coming from? The locals are gasping for cash like landed haddock.

Suddenly the mid-day ferry is glimpsed as a dot on the horizon. Everyone stirs and stands to attention in an orderly row and all eyes strain, even the sozzled ones. The ferry swells into view but halts and anchors offshore, riding on the waves while passengers transfer to the little red boat which will bring them to land at the jetty steps. We are scrutinising the commotion of bags, suitcases and bums for some outline of a plump man in his forties, with long dark hair and a pale face, wearing a beret. Could that be he? Or that one? No likely candidate presents himself. The red transit boat arrives at the jetty and ties up. As its passengers disembark – two priests and a telephone repairman – the remainder are sailors – Luca says 'Fuck...' and the camera, ready to immortalise Maruma's apprehensive face and transmit it to the world, slumps unused to his side on its straps. The islanders look at each other, shrug, and sit down more or less where they are and open more beer. Colin Carr gives a strangled asymmetrical laugh. Maruma has stood them up again. Yet again. No message of apology or explanation. Nothing. He simply didn't come, and if they still hope to see him the only thing they can do is – carry on waiting...

This resurgence of inertia is intolerable. Do we sit down and drink beer and utter vapidities until it's time to eat and get fatter? Not me. I escape up the hill to have a look inside the Protestant church. A shower breaks as I enter the neat Arts and Crafts building and when I come out again a perfect rainbow has arched from a field on the left into the sea on the right. The sun is warm on my head. Further up the lane the Huddersfield boy comes by on his motor scooter – he hadn't been waiting at the jetty, he had more sense. He points to the rainbow and looks at me and smiles. He knows the island well and tells me about an isolated tarn he likes to fish in. I ask him if we can go there and he says 'Sure'. We head for the centre of the island, leave the bike beside a stile, he unstraps his fishing rod, and we trek through heather, with the great tower of rock hanging over us like the sword of Damocles. It's too strenuous for conversation but at last we arrive at the dark pool of water, his special pond. The views are always immense on Eigg. But up here they are empyrean. As he joints together his rod, I try to take it in, the wheeling vistas, his expression concentrated on his fishing rod, the air passing clean through one's nostrils and lungs and blood, and instead of letting it go, letting it fly, letting it all disappear, I decide to ground it with an ordinary question. If I don't I might be blown away, never to return.

'Do you work on the island?'

'Oh no.'

I never, on principle, ask people what they do for a living, but I'm longing to know in his case, longing to decode his elfin grace, to find out exactly who he is. But I don't know what to say. He helps me by adding, with one eye screwed up, 'Don't work at anything much. Bit of this, bit of that.'

'Nothing you'd call a career.'

He smiles again. 'I'm too relaxed for a career.'

We sit quietly, making occasional small talk. Birds shriek high above us, gliding about the shaft of rock which is thick and black against the sky but cuts sharply into it because the sky, by contrast, is pure blue. He stands up, moves off a little into the heather for a pee and returns, buttoning the fascinating thing away. He's gifted with effortless, animal charm, but it doesn't work on the fish – nothing bites.

'Did you ever meet this German artist?' I ask.

'No. I heard about him. Don't you think he sounds like an idiot?'

Not an idiot, no. Maruma is a nightmare. People like Maruma, you have to avoid them. People who don't know whether they're coming or going. People who stand you up or cut you dead, and then express surprise if you're put out or hurt. Usually they're men unable to face it. Men more than women are guilty of offensive cowardice. Men are more easily discouraged than women. Maruma is frightened to come. If he's into fire energy it's probably because he has none himself. I'm willing to bet he's a water person who found himself the owner of Eigg not because of the volcanic plug driven through its heart but because it is an island, because it is surrounded and contained by water. If I were into astrology I'd wager he is a water sign – Cancer, Scorpio, Pisces – but I was never into astrology, not even when I was taking LSD, though that drug did give rise to an interest in numerology which is, I think, more credible since 'number' is what lies behind music and science. The only time I find my eyes wandering over the horoscopes in women's magazines is when I fall in love frustratedly, because then one is scanning the mythic realm for any signs, any clues, any way across the divide, any way out of the self and into the other, and so the irrational character of astrology becomes its recommendation, the loved one viewed with abstract objectivity from elsewhere.

Maruma is beginning to discover that a man who buys an island buys a kingdom, and that kingship is a trap. A king is not a free man, as Eigg's previous owner discovered. A trap but not a mistake. We may choose inconveniently or unwisely – for ourselves or for others – but we never choose incorrectly. We always gravitate to what we need to realise our particular natures. I think I'll phone Maruma again. But not from here, not from Eigg. I don't mind waiting for a while, for quite a long while very often. So much of my life has been spent waiting, because I don't see that there's any alternative if you are trying to achieve something. You get on with other things of course, but in your heart you are still waiting. For love, for success, for a cheque, for an answer, an acceptance, a telephone call, an email, a response, yes, a response, often that's all one is waiting for, a human response...But there comes a point when if you hang around any longer you're a berk.

So Luca and I packed our bags, said our good-byes, and caught the train from Mallaig to Glasgow. It was now, on the 16.10 train, that I had that freakish surprise. I found myself reading the actual obituary of Bapsy Pavry.

'Are you all right?' enquired Luca.

'I think so.'

'You look as though you've seen a ghost.'

No – the ghost was the obituary I'd read before. The precognition one. This was the real one – even more startling. It really was shocking to find that obituary exactly as I'd envisaged it, staring at me on the return train to Glasgow. Bapsy showing up again without warning.

Maybe Maruma will unexpectedly enter my life in the future, from an oblique angle, when it might take me a little time to register who the hell he is. I hope so.

In Glasgow we booked a suite for the night at the Central Hotel, a Victorian behemoth put up over the Central Railway Station and refitted in the 1930s with giant sofas and beds. Several huge rooms opened into each other before opening into a bathroom whose high Cunard curves disappeared in a blaze of white. Our sitting-room windows looked down on to the bustle of the station concourse which the double glazing transformed into a lively silent film. Viewed from the cushions of our gallery sofa, trains came and went in a bizarre silence. Luca wanted to snooze, so I took myself off to the health club in the basement and slotted myself into the sauna with one of the hotel waiters. He told me that the hotel had seen better days and that Laurel and Hardy, Frank Sinatra, Bob Hope, Churchill, the Kennedys and the Beach Boys had all stayed there. 'What about Cernuda?' I asked.

The heat hissed around his perplexity. He'd never heard of Cernuda. Few people have. I've never 'done' Glasgow. I'd like to one day. On this occasion it struck me as far more exciting than Edinburgh and soon after the Eigg jaunt I tried to arrange a visit to Glasgow in pursuit of Cernuda. He was a Spanish poet who was born in Seville in 1902. The first volume of his to make a mark was *Forbidden Pleasures* in 1931. Thereafter surrealism and classicism found a fruitful rapprochement in the work of a man who believed that 'he who knows love wants nothing else'. At the beginning of 1938 Cernuda left Spain to go on a lecture tour of England – and he never returned to his homeland. The triumph of Franco and the outbreak of the Second World War persuaded him to stay on as lecturer in Spanish studies at Glasgow University where he had gone in January 1939. He remained there until his move to Cambridge in 1944, London in 1945, the USA in 1947, and Mexico in 1952. Controversy surrounds his death in Mexico City in 1963 – some say it was a heart attack, others suicide after a rewarding love affair turned sour. The corollary of love eliminating all other needs is that when love goes you are left with nothing.

I rang the head of Hispanic Studies in the University of Glasgow, Professor Gareth Walters, to enquire whether any of Cernuda's colleagues might still be alive and he suggested I write to Neil McKinlay who was working on a study of Cernuda. Mr McKinlay said that Cernuda 'was very reclusive and loathed Glasgow intensely' but one of the Spaniard's colleagues, Ivy McClelland, was still alive. So I wrote to her. A letter came back – but from Professor Walters. 'Ivy does not feel she would have much to tell you about Cernuda as he was a very reserved person. She doubts it would be worthwhile for you to make a special visit to Glasgow to speak to her about him, but she will be willing to speak to you on the phone if you wish.' When I did ring her the phrases 'nothing to say', 'he was very reserved' went round and round, not a single personal observation of the man, let alone an anecdote. The page on which I was going to record my conversation with Ivy McClelland has one word on it: 'Nothing'.

A man by the name of Ian Gibson, writing to me on another matter in 1997, suggested I contact Rafael Martinez Nadal, a friend both of Lorca and Cernuda. Rafael lived in Hampstead, Mr Gibson said, and was very knowledgeable and approachable and in the telephone book. When I rang I learned that Mr Martinez Nadal was at his house in Madrid but would be back soon and I should write to him. I wrote a letter to the Hampstead address and was afterwards myself in Herefordshire – the South of France – St Petersburg – my father died – and there was no reply to my letter. Rafael Martinez Nadal died in 2001, aged 97.

•

Luca said 'I'm not going to Venice.'

'Copycat.'

'That's right. You convinced me. Next time I do a story I want to go somewhere hot. With brothels.'

'Try Mexico.'

'Definitely.'

In the end I think it was Nicaragua he went to – and never returned.

At least things were moving again. And we hadn't given up on Maruma altogether. Back in London, I tried the Maruma Centre repeatedly, with much the same result as before. He's running away while pretending not to run away; that's what this sort of person does unfortunately. Like old Monty did with Bapsy. Maruma's receptionist was always patient and good-natured. Occasionally she laughed and he was always unavailable: in a meeting, arriving later, anything to avoid confrontation. Until one day, right in the middle of her spiel, Maruma interrupted her and came on the line.

'Oh – you'll speak to me?'

'Yes.'

'About Eigg?'

'There are so many things going on at the moment, Duncan.'

You see, he's so damn nice. That's the other big problem with his kind – they're so damn nice. One is stymied by their niceness.

'What happens next, Maruma?'

'Long story.' I hear him inhale deeply on a fag.

'Well, what about the Lodge being turned into a health clinic?'

'There is shit energy there.'

'In the Lodge?'

'Yes.'

I'm surprised. I thought there was lovely energy there.

'Perhaps we will do hotel...'

Another go at the fag.

'And the proposed distillery? That would be popular. Fire-water.'

'What?'

'The red indians called alcohol fire-water.'

'...You see, I have to clean up so many misunderstandings caused by the press and I must especially clean them up with the people of Eigg.'

'Coz you're never there.'

'Yes, they cannot find out what person I am.'

This is the nub of it, isn't it. Why is communication such an act of bravery? Why do we hide the truth that is in our hearts? Oh, the truth! No arrangement ever came about by telling the truth. People often prefer to die than to tell the truth, hoping that a more acceptable truth will arrive in the future, one that they can admit to.

But truth is really all that matters because the great thing is to be able to look someone in the eye. The truth is nakedness now. The truth is active. And not telling the truth is what paralyses everything.

'So why don't you go there and reveal yourself?' I ask.

Sigh.

'Do you have money problems?'

'I have no money problems.'

'Do you love the island?'

'Yes, I fell in love with it when I saw it from above.'

'And from below?'

'Below?'

'Is it too much for you on the ground?'

'I don't understand,' he says.

He's choking. I feel awful really, goading him on.

'Are you afraid of Eigg now?'

'No, not afraid. But I don't want to play the landlord.'

'Unless you play the landlord, nothing will happen.'

'What would you like to do with Eigg?'

'Me?'

He's asking me. There *is* something enchanting about him.

'Yes, Duncan, you. You seem very interested. So have you got any ideas what to do with it?' I hear him light another cigarette–in Stuttgart.

'Well, yes, actually. I do have some ideas.'

'Which you believe in?'

'I said ideas. Not beliefs.'

I don't have beliefs. Beliefs are dead things. I want to know things, not believe things. I have some ideas I could propose, that's all.

'We must talk more about this, face to face, on Eigg.'

Oh dear, we've been here before.

'Definitely. Yes. When will you visit it next?' I enquire flatly.

'Soon I hope. Maybe at the end of the month.'

'Or at the beginning of next?'

'Yes...'

So the islanders waited and waited. I didn't wait, no siree, not any more. But they had no choice. They waited. Ends of months and beginnings of months came and went. And they waited for their lover to answer their appeals, to call, to speak, to visit. And still they waited, unable to move forwards or to have closure or to grasp what on earth was going on, fettered by his remoteness and his refusal and his silence. They never saw any more of Maruma. He never returned. Then one day the island was put up for sale. And the islanders raised the money to buy it for themselves. They need never wait for a lover again.

CHAPTER FOUR

Who was
Alastair Graham?

At the end of the nineteen-seventies I was living in the small town of Hay-on-Wye writing a book. Several times a week it was necessary to escape Hay's delightful, gossipy confines, and one of my jaunts took me to New Quay. This is not to be confused with Newquay in Cornwall, surf capital of Britain; and it not often is because New Quay is an obscure fishing village on the west coast of Wales. Its brightly painted cottages have storm porches of coloured glass and are built in terraces on cliffs of black rock. Beneath them, coves of pebbles alternate with loops of dull sand. In the season, not very well-off holidaymakers occupy its few modest hotels and boarding houses.

It was not the season. It was chilly and damp and the sky was a monotonous grey. At lunchtime, after meandering New Quay's little streets, I entered a pub called the Dolau Inn not far from the sulky, flapping water. There was a mere handful of customers inside and, having ordered a pint, I nodded at a character sitting on a high stool at the end of the bar and eventually exchanged a few words with him. He was getting on in years and bald, with a trim grey beard, and dressed spotlessly in yachting clothes: sailcloth trousers with knife-edge creases, a navy-blue jersey, slip-on deck shoes. One thing struck me in particular: his nails, perfectly manicured, were white from base to tip. His hands looked as though they'd never touched even so much as a tiller (an erroneous impression, it turned out). In these simple surroundings his curiosity lay chiefly in the air he had of an extreme refinement tinged with exoticism.

He was also a nervous fellow and our conversation, such as it was, never flowed. He held his head down bashfully and from time to time, when speaking, cast blue lugubrious eyes upwards from beneath a lowered brow. The voice, issuing from slightly pursed lips, was fastidious but not affected, and his manner of expression had that casual charm which suggests a great deal and is utterly unrevealing.

I told him that I'd abandoned London the previous year after coming unstuck. He said he'd done the same thing but long, long ago and hadn't been back, 'except briefly during the Suez crisis.'

'Why did you leave?'

'Because I'd had enough!'

He fingered the beer mat to distract himself from this sudden show of temperament.

'So why did you return during the Suez crisis?'

'I'd had some experience of that part of the world. I think they thought I could help.'

'And could you?'

'Could anyone?'

Shuffling about for a change of subject, I mentioned that I was reading Joseph Conrad and rereading the early novels of Evelyn Waugh. The beer mat did a couple of rapid twirls. He said he used to love Conrad. I said that I thought that the more serious Waugh's tone became, the worse his writing was. My companion nodded. When I advanced the idea that although well-endowed as a writer, Waugh's later work was undermined by the progressive narrowing of his sympathies, the old man uttered an extraordinary remark.

'He wasn't well-endowed in the other sense, I'm afraid.' How on earth had that gear-change come about? He could see I was taken aback; but having quipped, he remained silent, staring at his Cinzano on the rocks, as though he'd surprised himself too. Could his reference to Waugh's private parts have been a way of making a pass? I thought I'd find out and asked 'What do you mean exactly?', at which he waffled something in a low tone which I simply didn't grasp and courteously excused himself, saying he had to get back for lunch. We shook hands, he said good-bye to the landlord, with whom he was on easy polite terms (the landlord called him Mr Graham), slid away in those perfect clothes, and that was that.

·

A few months later I was having dinner with a friend of mine, Nick Jones-Evans, at his house. Nick lives in Presteigne on the Welsh Marches forty minutes north of Hay. His family used to own property in New Quay and he spoke of some arcane leasehold arrangement concerning a chapel there. So I mentioned my visit and particularly of my meeting with the funny old gent.

'Ah,' said Nick, 'I think I know who that was. I met him myself once, years ago, in my teens. That was also in the Dolau. I was with my father and when I started talking to him, my father called me away. When we got outside he said "You mustn't talk to that man again. He's well-bred – but unclean". The thing I always remember is that his nails were so highly polished I thought he must've been wearing nail varnish. We talked about the film *A Clockwork Orange* which he'd recently seen and was very interested in.'

'But who is he?'

'He's called Graham somebody and arrived in the district before the war with a retinue of servants and, the rumour went, ten thousand a year. But he was always considered a dubious character. I wish I'd made more of a stab at getting to know him.'

'He told me that Evelyn Waugh had a small cock.'

'Goodness me – did he say more about it than that?'

'No, he didn't. But the pub landlord called him Mr Graham.'

'That's it, Alastair Graham. I did hear once that he'd had a fling with a New Quay postman. Now look, you've got to finish that fish pie. I did it specially for you.'

•

Two years later, living in London again, I was talking one afternoon to Charles Sturridge at a friend's flat in Linden Gardens. He was directing the television series of *Brideshead Revisited* and said 'The great mystery is – where is the real Sebastian Flyte? The model for the character was someone called Alastair Graham. Waugh met him at Oxford and they were lovers in the Twenties. Then after leading an interesting life, Graham suddenly vanished from the scene in the Thirties. We don't know where and we don't know why.'

You may recall that Sebastian Flyte is the youthful drunkard with whom the narrator of *Brideshead Revisited* falls in love when they are undergraduates together at Oxford. Charles was full of the show and soon moved on from the mysteries of Graham to the wonders of directing Laurence Olivier. At the time nothing registered. So great was the disparity between the two images – young radiant Lord Sebastian Flyte and the jittery old codger in the pub – that it wasn't until the following week that I recalled my seaside encounter years before, and the penny dropped, and I realised that although I didn't know why, I certainly knew where. Sebastian Flyte was living in New Quay.

•

Naturally I wished to return there, establish contact and discover his story, particularly to find out what had made him run away at such an early age from everything he knew. Meanwhile Charles Sturridge arranged for his television company to do a search of the printed sources and send me the results. They amounted to quite a stack of pages, much of it from Evelyn Waugh's diaries, and with the help of this preliminary material I was able to pencil an outline profile.

Graham was born in 1904 and went to Brasenose College, Oxford in 1922, that memorable year of Eliot's *The Waste Land*, Joyce's *Ulysses*, Wittgenstein's *Tractatus*, the death of Proust and the opening of Le Boeuf sur le Toit, the first modern nightclub. Graham drank too much, failed his exams, and came down in 1923. He and Waugh were constantly together at Barford House in Warwickshire to which Graham's mother, who was called Jessie, had moved. After her son's flop at the University, Mrs Graham enrolled the boy in an architectural school in London but he never attended any of its classes. Next he became an apprentice at the Shakespeare Head Press at Stratford, where he published Waugh's first work, an essay on the Pre-Raphaelites, but that didn't last either. In 1928 he joined the Diplomatic Service – and left it in 1933. End of career. No more jobs. All this sounds perfunctory and disjointed, and one gets the impression that these activities occurred spasmodically, against a background of drifting and boozing which were the really coherent activities. Obviously Graham had dropped out before he was thirty years old. But the question is – had he ever dropped in?

Waugh in his autobiography *A Little Learning* gives Graham the name 'Hamish Lennox'. In a book of very many names, only two others are deemed so sensitive as to require aliases ('Preters' and 'Captain Grimes'). Waugh calls Graham *the friend of my heart*. And for a number of years...*we were inseparable or, if separated, in almost daily communication...Hamish's home was uncongenial to him. His father, the younger son of a Border family, was dead and his mother was high-tempered, possessive, jolly and erratic...*

This mother was an American and came to be (Waugh wrote) the model for Lady Circumference in *Decline and Fall*. In his autobiography Waugh also mentions, misleadingly, that his friend went to live abroad and became a recluse – taken together these remarks imply that Graham hid overseas from some threat. In *Brideshead Revisited*, his fate is worse. Sebastian Flyte lives with a German boyfriend in Morocco and Athens but after the German later hangs himself in a Nazi camp, Sebastian drifts back to North Africa, collapses into permanent alcoholism and sickness, and is taken in by a monastery near Tunis where he scuffs about as an under-porter and dies.

And that was all on Alastair Graham. He wasn't even mentioned in Marie-Jacqueline Lancaster's *Brian Howard: Portrait of a Failure*, an otherwise fairly comprehensive dossier of Oxfordian shenanigans in the nineteen-twenties. After 1933 Graham's trail disappeared completely. Even those in the know didn't know what had happened to him.

Does it matter? Well, it's tantalising. Recluses and absconders always are. They bring out the mischief in one as well as the curiosity. You suddenly ran away, old fruit, and have been hiding for fifty years. We want to know why. Something unsavoury no doubt. Also the story of this Anglo-American misfit is the only piece missing from the otherwise well documented Brideshead Generation. Graham is its most shadowy figure and yet the one most important to Waugh himself. Their correspondence, perhaps lying in a Welsh drawer alongside thick photograph albums, would be of great importance, especially as Waugh destroyed his Oxford diary claiming, in an hysterical tone, that it recorded a period during which he was 'quite incredibly depraved morally'.

And so I decided to return to the seaside village of New Quay and call on Alastair Graham and invite him out to dinner. No harm in that–surely? It was October 1981; I drove across England to Presteigne and asked Nick Jones-Evans to accompany me for support. He had a good idea–*Burke's Peerage*–and we combed his 1938 edition. Alastair Hugh Graham was listed under Graham of Netherby, a baronetcy in Cumberland. His father, Hugh Graham, died on November 25th 1921, the year before his son went to Oxford, and as a result one presumes Alastair came wholly under the influence of the possessive mother. No wonder he drank.

According to *Burke's Peerage*, which incorporates detailed genealogies, Alastair Graham's mother, Jessie, was a daughter of Andrew Low of Savannah, Georgia, and she died in 1934. This was the year after Graham's vanishing act. His father's sisters – Alastair's aunts - were the Duchess of Montrose, the Countess of Verulam and Lady Wittenham. Grander than one had expected.

Alastair had a brother and a sister who both died young. A second sister, Sibyl, married a farmer in Kenya in 1920. So it also turned out to have been a family of many unhappy losses. Alastair was listed in 1938 as owning a house called Wern Newydd in New Quay as well as Barford, his mother's old place in Warwickshire. She'd been dead for four years but he still kept Barford on, which struck me as curious.

'Wern Newydd sounds quite big,' said Nick, 'which would explain the retinue of servants we all heard about.'

Next day Nick and I drove to the coast and booked into the New Quay Hotel. Nick was wearing his tweed cape and deerstalker and also smoking a pipe. He quite often does but on this occasion the Sherlock Holmes get-up was absurdly appropriate. As usual on the west coast of Wales, the weather was windy and drizzly. The first thing we discovered, I think from the proprietor of our hotel, was that Alastair Graham no longer lived at Wern Newydd, which was in the countryside nearby. He now lived in New Quay proper, in Rock Street which was a row of stone cottages above the harbour. Graham inhabited Number 8.

We trudged over to the Dolau Inn where there was a major setback.

'You used to be able to time your clock by Mr Graham. But he hardly ever comes by these days. He hasn't been well. And he won't let you in. Round here we call his house the Kremlin.'

Perhaps it was naïve to expect someone who'd deliberately withdrawn from society to give a welcome to strangers – and 'Kremlin'? It sounded dreadful. But undeterred and optimistic, we walked over to Rock Street and to number 8 which was the finest in the row, double-fronted, painted dark pink, with an eighteenth-century porch. A dolphin stood on either side of the entrance. I knocked on the front door which was blue. There was a long interval. Nick and I looked at each other nervously. At last there was the sound of a lock being turned and the jangle of a chain being disengaged. The door opened sheepishly, a third of the way. Those blue sad eyes, which I recognised at once, peered over a pair of spectacles in steady, watery silence. It was the same old man I'd met in the pub years before, the same trim beard, the same freshly pressed nautical clothes and blue deck shoes. Not very tall. But he looked much thinner. There was no 'Can I help you?' from him, nor even a 'Yes?'. Only a stare. So I said please forgive us for calling like this and I introduced Nick and myself, mentioning that actually we'd met before, and I explained my interest in Evelyn Waugh and the nineteen-twenties – whereupon he started to flap like a cornered bird and became quite desperate.

'I've had a stroke, I can't remember anything, I've nothing to say!' His eyes registered even greater consternation as he caught sight of Nick's Sherlock Holmes outfit.

I was stumped. For some reason a response as abrupt as this had never crossed my mind. I've used the word 'naïve' but a better one would be 'innocent'. I'd been innocent.

I considered my interest in history, literature and life to be entirely legitimate and in need of no special pleading. How wrong I was. I played another card: 'Would you like to join us for dinner this evening?' In the circumstances it sounds bloody mad, put down like that, and his reaction was worse still.

'Oh, no! I can't go out, I'm not fit to be seen! I had a stroke last year, I'm an invalid, I can't think at all, everything was so long ago – he was older than me, you know.'

Well - that last observation of his popped out oddly, accompanied by something slightly less frantic in the eyes. 'He was older than me, you know.' What on earth was going on in his head? It suggested guilt, an attempt to transfer responsibility for something bad. Graham, his eyes having now attached themselves to the polished door-knob, began to fiddle with it – he was too well brought up to slam the door in our faces. He had slender, beetroot-red hands, with those fingernails of deathly white, no pink in them, which I'd noticed at our first encounter.

'But weren't you Sebastian Flyte?' I blurted out, now in some disarray myself.

He flinched back into the hall. 'No, not me, not me – er, it was a friend of mine.'

'But Waugh said it was you.' I blundered appallingly on. 'And in the original manuscript of *Brideshead Revisited* Waugh wrote Alastair instead of Sebastian'.

'Please, no, I'm an invalid, I can't remember anything.'

One could tell from the intense clarity of the eyes that he had all his wits and could remember everything. But it was pathetic. His whole demeanour was of a man in mortal fear of exposure. It was impossible to persist and I apologised, wished him well, and came away thoroughly embarrassed. But one had to give it a try. If you are drawn by something or someone, you have to give it a try. Rejection is hurtful but not even trying is worse. I'd foreseen a charming harbourside dinner while Graham reminisced flavoursomely to a pair of fans; old people are usually happy to talk to younger people about their lives, rarely having much opportunity to do so. Instead of that it had been a disaster and I was acutely ashamed of myself.

Nick felt as shabby as I, but added 'Did you see inside?'

'No.'

'Marvellous stuff.'

While I'd been trying to engage Graham, Nick–who is extremely tall–had been rubber-necking behind me and had missed little. Icons in the hall, chandeliers too big for the rooms, gilded furniture, old polished wood, a Georgian bracket clock, roped curtains. 'And very very clean,' added Nick.

'But that terrible remark of his.'

'Which one?'

'I'm not fit to be seen. It sent a chill down my spine.'

'Well, he wasn't very attractive.'

'You know that's not what I meant.'

It so happened that Alastair Graham's housekeeper worked part-time in the bar of our hotel and that evening we met her. Her name was Lottie Evans. She was guarded but not closed-up, and she told us that every day except Sundays she went into Mr Graham's at 10 am until twelve. She'd been housemaid under the housekeeper Mrs Cooke at the big house, the Wern, when Graham lived there.

'Mr Graham has books sent up from London,' said

Lottie, 'and reads all the time, in the back–he never uses the front two rooms, always in the back he is.'

'Why do you think he abandoned his life and retired here while still a young man?'

At this she did clam up and confessed that she didn't feel happy about saying anything more. Generally speaking the remarks of the locals wove an uneasy secretiveness around Alastair Graham, so that he gradually became a figure touched more by tragedy than by scandal. Nick and I drove past his old house, Wern Newyyd, two miles out of New Quay on the left. A stone mansion with twin gables, hunkered down in a gulley among woods as though trying to bury itself. Both the house and its setting were timelessly beautiful, as far away from everything as a man could get.

•

Back in London, I muckraked with negligible results. However I did by chance speak to Claud Cockburn only weeks before his death in November 1981.

'Alastair was a roaring Roman Catholic when I knew him,' said Claud. 'He had a car called Zazou which broke down. We opened the bonnet but neither of us knew anything about mechanics. In frustration Alastair struck the thing with a spanner and said "We must pray". A muscular Protestant British parson happened to come by and asked "Anything I can do?" Alastair said "We're praying" and the parson said "I can't see that'll do much good" and went on his way. Alastair hated towns, except for Venice. He adored Venice. Before the war anyway. I don't know where he went after the war. When was the last time I saw him? In Tangier in 1936, and I was struck by his complete indifference to the Spanish Civil War, then at its height. After that he simply disappeared.'

Claud Cockburn was always amazed by anyone not as totally hung up on Spain as he was - it was while in Madrid that Claud fucked Isherwood's 'Sally Bowles' (Jean Ross) and gave her a daughter.

•

January 1983. Nick Jones-Evans telephoned to say that he'd heard from an acquaintance on the coast that Graham had died the previous autumn 'taking his secrets with him'. To Nick's knowledge there had been no sale and he didn't know what had happened to Graham's papers.

February 25th 1983. I was having dinner with Harold Acton at La Pietra, his house above Florence. Waugh had dedicated his first novel *Decline and Fall* to Harold and I told him of Graham's death.

'How extraordinary that you can tell me that,' he remarked. 'It really is extraordinary, because not a single one of his contemporaries would have known it. I didn't know him well because he kept to himself. I don't think anyone knew him well except Evelyn. I can say he was very good-looking in a delicate Pre-Raphaelite way and had the same sort of features as Evelyn liked in girls. The pixie look. He was not a hearty but he dressed like a hearty, in the country style, plus-fours and *tweeds*.' Harold, also an Anglo-American, gave me a twinkly eye as he used that word 'tweeds', always his classic put-down.

'And although Graham was rather quiet,' he continued,

'he drank like a fish. I believe the mother was part of the problem. She is portrayed in Evelyn's story, Winner Takes All'. (This is Mrs Kent-Cumberland, another of Waugh's Red Queen women. She is less amusing and nastier than Lady Circumference.)

'Oh yes, he and Evelyn were always together,' mused Harold with an odd smile. 'An infatuation. And it went on for quite a few years. We hardly saw anything of Evelyn at that time. Oh, definitely an infatuation.'

Harold of course was in *Brideshead Revisited* too. He and Brian Howard were blended in 'Anthony Blanche', the aesthete of Christ Church. So momentarily – ha! – I was listening to Anthony Blanche's sly complaint, sixty years after the event, that Sebastian Flyte had stolen the narrator Charles Ryder from him.

•

The Graham trail petered out. I lost interest. Until one day I found myself in Warwickshire, on the road between Leamington Spa and Stratford-upon-Avon. It was one of those spacious, wintry English days – bit cold, bit windy, bit wet – which combine pensive and tonic qualities. I noticed a sign which said 'Barford'. It was a few moments before its significance registered – oh yes, Barford – Barford House was where Alastair had lived with his mother all those years ago – whereupon an inquisitiveness welled up strongly and I decided to turn off. Suddenly I wanted to see Graham's boyhood home and the scene of Evelyn Waugh's youthful imagination. I wanted to go back seventy years.

I've searched my annual diaries, which are for

appointments (which I keep) and dates of parties (which I may or may not got to), and I've searched my journals which are sketchy not systematic, and simply cannot establish what year this was, the year of my fortuitous visit to Barford. But it must have been in the late nineteen-eighties. Certainly before the coming of the M40. Since my visit, the M40 extension has been constructed alongside the village and more or less seen off the place. But in the late 1980s Barford, when finally I reached it via serpentine lanes, was still peaceful and at a distance from things. Barford House was on the edge of the village and the first surprise was that it wasn't at all in the stately-home class and was quite close to the road. It was a substantial white stucco building embellished with Ionic half-columns on the front and a picturesque conservatory to the left. The second surprise was that like Brideshead Castle, and Castle Howard which was used in the television series, it had a dome and lantern on the roof above the centre, albeit on a modest scale. Waugh, who was passionate about architecture, would have registered everything.

It was 3.30 in the afternoon. Children were trailing home from school with satchels and rucksacks, but though near the roadway, the house was apart from such traffic, screened by a mature stand of evergreen trees. I hovered for a while at the entrance to the drive, hoping to see someone, but the house was lifeless, as though its heart stopped for ever when the Grahams and the Waughs of this world went away. No clue as to its present occupancy was discernible and, after the slap in New Quay, I was disinclined to knock, uninvited and unknown, on its front door (and I've never done so anywhere again!). But the visit to

Barford did rekindle my interest in the fate of Alastair Graham. Perhaps now that he'd died, people would talk more freely.

At home in Notting Hill I took out the dusty file and browsed its contents. I thought I might as well quiz those two stalwarts of memory lane, Anthony Powell and Peter Quennell, and yes, they both remembered Graham from Oxford and like everyone else used the phrase 'good-looking' – 'extremely good-looking,' emphasised Powell, 'with rather Dresden china shepherdess sort of looks.' And also like everyone else who'd known him in the 1920s, they knew nothing of his whereabouts since that time. I could see that Alastair Graham's evanescence was part of his appeal and originality.

Selina Hastings came up with something solid: two surviving letters from Alastair to Evelyn. She thought there were no others but I managed to unearth a third – where from? Oh yes, Auberon Waugh copied it for me from the Waugh archive. All three are unpublished and undated but from the period 1922–25. The most evocative is the Burgundy letter sent from London in 1923 or 24, addressed to Waugh at Hertford College, Oxford. Enclosed with it is a photograph of Alastair standing naked on a rock with what appears to be a waterfall in the background. Whether Alastair himself put the photograph there, or Evelyn did later on, was uncertain (Bron said). It was one of the few things from this period that Waugh, despite the later virulence of his religion, couldn't bear to destroy. The letter reads:

Saturday

My dear Evelyn,

I'm sending this down by David or the Bastard John, whom I'm seeing this evening. I am sad that you wouldn't come up for this party. I am afraid it will be bloody. One can always drink but it is rather a cheap path to heaven. I've found the ideal way to drink Burgundy. You must take a peach and peal [sic] it, and put it in a finger bowl, and pour the Burgundy over it. The flavour is exquisite. And the peach seems to exaggerate that delightful happy Seraglio contentedness that old wine evokes. An old French lady taught it to me, who has a wonderful cellar at Lavalles. I've been in bed with pains in my ears for the last two days. May I go and call on your parents one day, or would they hate it? I do not know whether I ought to come to Oxford or not next week. It depends on money and other little complications. If I come, will you come and drink with me somewhere? on Saturday. If it is a nice day we might carry some bottles into a wood or some bucolic place, and drink like Horace. I'm afraid this is a poor wandering letter. But I cannot write letters. It was only meant to express my sorrow at your absence from this party. I wish you felt merrier, and were not so serious.

With love from Alastair, and his poor dead heart.

The tone of whimsy and sad sweetness is so exactly that of Sebastian Flyte that it is clearer than ever how much of

Alastair's stripling manner was the basis for that character. Not to mention the outing to drink 'some bottles' in the countryside – such an outing on a sunny summer's day is the first magical set piece in *Brideshead Revisited*.

Another of the letters to Waugh, sent from The Bury, Offchurch, Leamington, probably in 1925, contains these telling lines:

> …all the beautiful things that I have seen, heard or thought of, grow like bright flowers and musky herbs in a garden where I can enjoy their presence, and where I can sit in peace and banish the unpleasant things of life. A kind of fortified retreat that no one can enter except myself.

Both Narcissus and the recluse are glimpsed in these letters but of course narcissism and reclusiveness are profoundly linked: you can gaze into your pool only so long as you are undisturbed by others.

Alastair's brief diplomatic foray was the most active period of his life and also marks the final phase with Waugh. It is, like everything else, largely unrecorded. But I scavenged every possible source – journals, letters, forgotten autobiographies – and feel reasonably confident in putting together the following.

He had begun to travel independently soon after leaving Oxford, partly to avoid his mother, partly to explore his sexuality. While homosexuality was illegal in England and America, the Mediterranean was the place for Anglo-Saxon gay men to escape to, and Tangier, Ibiza, Capri, Taormina, Florence, Rome, Mykonos, Tunis, the South of France, became enticing destinations largely on account of allowing misfits of all kinds to breathe more easily and be themselves. Germany provided a more specialised release for Auden and Isherwood, Egypt and India for E. M. Forster, China for Harold Acton: the list could go on and on. Curiously the situation has now in many respects reversed. As the Anglo-Saxon world has developed a high degree of lifestyle diversity, people from other cultures, especially from the Islamic world, flock to it to escape the crushing conformism of their own societies. Yet the Mediterranean still retains its air of liberating, sensual sunshine. Waugh's *The Ordeal of Gilbert Pinfold* (1957) is a thinly disguised account of his nervous breakdown and it is his most honest book. In it he calls the Mediterranean 'that splendid enclosure which held all the world's history and half the happiest memories of his own life; of work and rest and battle, of aesthetic adventure and of young love.'

Although I do not particularly feel a misfit myself, I'm not terribly excited by conventional company. I find people who don't 'fit in' attractive and, on reflection, I discover that all my important lovers have been eccentric in some way. But in the fuller sense, everyone has their misfit aspect – philosophers have called it the human condition – and we are each of us embarked on an unpredictable journey. Is this especially true in our age of dislocation which some call globalisation? One could go further and suggest that 'fitting in' can seem like suffocation in the twenty-first century. The idea that one's background (class, culture, language, country) is irrelevant is absurd, and yet increasing numbers of people do resent being detained or described by their origins in any way. So there is conflict, because the whole world is hung up on two lies: that we are all the same, that we are all different. But we were warned. At the root of Western literature is *The Iliad* which is about leaving one's home to go out into the world and realise oneself in the battle of life. Only after, as a sequel, comes *The Odyssey*, the attempt to return, the wandering search for home once again – and hoping to recognise it when you find it. These great seminal books told us long ago: expect to be surprised by the human adventure, expect to be hurt, expect to be moved, upset, mirthful, angry; and give love, find love.

Alastair's voyaging generally took him to 'the Levant', which to-day one thinks of as those lands on the eastern shore of the Mediterranean. But in the nineteen-twenties the word might connote Greece, Crete, Cyprus, and also Malta which was the staging post for Tunis. The Levant was particularly fashionable at the time and one may ascribe this not only to Muslim bisexuality and to the adventures of Lawrence of Arabia during the Great War but also, in our more strictly literary circle, to E. M. Forster having intro-duced Cavafy to a British readership in *Pharos and Pharil-lon* (1923). Moving around the Levant in the 1920s were William Plomer, Steven Runciman, Robert Byron, Mark Ogilvie-Grant, David Talbot Rice and his wife Tamara. A group of them, including Alastair, had a riotous party in Istanbul 1933 on the night that Ataturk banned the wearing of the fez for men (he'd banned the wearing of the veil for women some years earlier).

It was Steven Runciman above all who made the area his own. He has written seductively of his youthful arriv-als there on the Orient Express, taking the train from

Calais to Salonika to Istanbul, though he never so much as hinted at his *amours* (concerning which he was agonisingly bashful – his memoirs plumb new depths of sexlessness, although I did learn from them that Runciman had also been stormbound in Catania port for two days, on his grandfather's yacht in 1924). When I was an undergraduate in 1968, I used the Orient Express on the same route as Runciman. By then it was on its last legs – or wheels – and would soon disappear altogether, but there was still an old Ottoman dining car attached which was enough to make one's breakfast of rolls, goat's cheese and coffee a highly romantic experience. As we steamed into Istanbul railway station, I remember looking out of the window and seeing a corpse beside the tracks partially obscured by windblown newspapers, and thinking 'Ah, this is life!'

When Waugh arrived in Athens at Christmas 1926, Graham was established there in a modern flat with Leonard Bower, an attaché at the British Embassy. Waugh wrote in his diary: 'The flat is usually full of dreadful Dago youths called by heroic names such as Miltiades or Agamemnon with blue chins and greasy clothes who sleep with the English colony for 25 drachmas a night'.

Also with them in Athens was a man with a red beard who kept trying to seduce Alastair. In the published Waugh *Diaries* his name is given as R–. Thinking that this man might provide a further lead, I called the Humanities Research Centre at Austin in Texas where the *Diaries* are lodged. They really are terrifically on the ball in Texas – the relevant entry was read back to me over the phone. The man's name turned out to be Arthur Reade and Waugh 'used to meet him in my Great Ormond Street, 1917 Club days'. It didn't mean anything at the time but I've now googled 'Arthur Reade'. Very little. He's called Britain's first Trotskyist, and the 1917 Club was a Communist hangout in Gerrard Street, Soho, not Great Ormond Street. Has anyone else picked up on this flirtation of Waugh's with Communism? Or am I the last to know?

I explored the Foreign Office papers at the Public Record Office because on February 20th 1928, Alastair became personal assistant to the British ambassador in Athens, Sir Percy Loraine. Presumably in consequence, he was not present at Waugh's marriage to Evelyn Gardner in June of that year at St Paul's, Portman Square. Or had Waugh actually not invited him? The occasion was hardly 'a wedding'; no parents were there; Harold Acton was best man and generously paid for the lunch at Boulestin afterwards.

Waugh was impoverished but managed to cruise to the Levant in February 1929 on a travel book commission. His wife developed double pneumonia and went into hospital at Port Said where she almost died. Alastair, answering he said Waugh's 'pathetic cry for help', arrived from Athens and gave Waugh £50. He often gave Waugh money and four years earlier, in 1925, had guaranteed Waugh's overdraft—to Mrs Graham's great displeasure. For two days Alastair and Evelyn did the low life of Port Said together and it was reported that the new Mrs Waugh resented being abandoned in favour of the former lover. One of the hallucinated voices in *Pinfold* raises the issue nearly thirty years later: 'I want the truth, Pinfold. *What were you doing* in Egypt in 1929?' Whatever it was, it can't have been insuperable because Mr and Mrs Waugh followed Graham back to

Greece for an interlude, and in May 1929 Waugh was writing to Henry Yorke from Istanbul that he and his wife had 'fun at Athens with Mark & Alastair.'

When Sir Percy Loraine became British High Commissioner in Cairo, Alastair went along too, being appointed honorary attaché at the Residency on September 2nd 1929. Technically a kingdom, Egypt had in effect been a British protectorate since 1883 (thus making Cecil Rhodes's great dream come true: it was possible to travel the length of Africa, from Cape Town to Alexandria, without leaving British territory). Mark Ogilvie-Grant was appointed to a similar post on December 2nd. A third character, Vivian Cornelius, was appointed honorary attaché on January 10th 1930. Ogilvie-Grant had his 'appointment terminated' in November 1932. Cornelius 'resigned' May 1933. Alastair had his 'appointment terminated' in December 1933. Again, all this information is from the Foreign Office papers. The phrase 'appointment terminated' is not necessarily ignominious. It was often applied to contract officers, as opposed to career diplomats, when their employment ended. It's too late presumably to speak to Mr Cornelius about those days.

It was the following year, on May 13th 1934, that Alastair's mother died. His father he had loved, and lost while still a teenager. His mother, who was richer than the father, he'd more or less detested but she'd been the only pressure on his life for action. With her gone he appears to have lost a drive and a shield. The drive he could do without; he had his inheritance. The shield he would replace by other means. And of course he no longer had to go abroad to escape her. One thing is clear: by this time

Evelyn Waugh was no longer in Alastair's life. The last notice I could trace of them together is at Pakenham Hall in Ireland, 1930 – Alastair talked of Abyssinia, sowing the seeds of *Remote People* and *Black Mischief* – although Waugh did write to Daphne Fielding in 1962 (year of the first Beatles' single!) that he hadn't seen Alastair for twenty-five years which, if precise, would make their last meeting in 1937. But I don't think Waugh was being precise; he was being vague.

Waugh's horror of the banal, his need to make all events participate in his personal mythology, can lead to misrepresentations. Yet one of the most fascinating aspects of his genius is the transformation of facts into fictions. This tempering of his imagination by fact gives his work a rare quality of combining extravagance with leanness, always an irresistible combination. Perhaps I was wrong in my remark to Alastair Graham about Waugh's work being undermined by his narrowing sympathies. Perhaps Waugh has the art to survive his own vileness and snobbery – because he was of course an artist. We should not make the mistake, which Waugh makes, of trying to judge him as a gentleman. And for Waugh, man and artist, Alastair Graham had by 1930 served his purpose.

There is a notion that having made grand connections at Oxford, Waugh's life thereafter was replete with titles and great houses. This wasn't so. In order to be at ease among the *gratin* he needed money and recognition as an artist and these did not come immediately. And it was only in the artier, more dysfunctional area of the upper class that he made his friends and was comfortable. The mainstream grandees of the peerage or the international set were not his territory. Diana Mitford, for example, said later that she was bewildered when Waugh suddenly broke off their close friendship in 1930 – she never realised that because she had become, as Diana Guinness, very rich and one of the most glamorous women in Europe, Waugh simply couldn't cope.

Waugh's essential move was to escape from his parents' house in Golders Green. Which took a long time. He often returned to live with them from necessity – in 1935 he's living there again. Meanwhile he adopted a series of alternative families. Waugh could not approach the aristocracy directly, especially when after Oxford he found himself teaching in second-rate schools for a pittance. He needed a less intimidating bridge, some middleground in which to groom his personality and manners, in which to learn without being overpowered.

It was the Graham household at Barford which supplied the perfect reductionist model of country-house style. The house itself wasn't huge but it had all the right things. Alastair himself wasn't one of the landed Etonians and, like Waugh, he'd gone to a Victorian school; yet he was a good-looking and dissolute member of the gentry class, which gave him the allure of decadence. Most important of all, there was no father in the household to make Waugh uneasy and put him on his mettle. So at Barford he could enjoy his upper-class fantasy without being threatened. During the period of humiliation as a schoolmaster, it was also his escape, enabling him to preserve caste in his own eyes. And the whole affair with Alastair confirmed which direction Waugh would take when he emerged from his shell and became his own man: it would be provincial county, not Harold Acton cosmopolitan. Graham was never much interested in London, but nor was he interested in traditional country pursuits. For him the countryside was a refuge, as Waugh hoped it would be for him too. In this Graham was the more successful. Waugh never found a refuge anywhere.

By the 1930s Waugh was ready to graduate to the much larger Madresfield Court where again there was no *paterfamilias* to intimidate the atmosphere. Lord Beauchamp, father of the seven Lygon children, was forced into exile in Italy in 1931 by his brother-in-law the Duke of Westminster, the philistine 'Bendor'. The Duke's personality was an odd mixture of prudery and passion (his mistress for many years was Coco Chanel and Simon Blow tells me that he gave Coco what a private note calls 'a sexual illness': the Duke was too embarrassed to deal with it and asked Detmar Blow to go and pacify her). This mixture came fully into play when he discovered that his brother-in-law Beauchamp enjoyed sleeping with his own sex, especially with footmen. This was not an uncommon practice but Bendor was a bully too. Prised away by the Duke threatening to expose her husband, Lady Beauchamp fled to the protection of her brother, leaving Madresfield in the hands of her offspring. It was this state of affairs which enabled Waugh to move in on them. While staying in Malvern he made contact and complained that he had nowhere to go for Christmas, which got him invited to Madresfield Court, a house he'd never before seen. Waugh preferred classical architecture but Madresfield's array of turrets and battlements would do. He later said that the place looked like an orphanage – which in a way it was.

Hugh Lygon, Lord Beauchamp's younger son, is sometimes touted as the model for Sebastian Flyte but there are only technical similarities. Waugh wasn't particularly close to him at Oxford and was not among those invited to Hugh's 21st birthday party. Hugh lacked Graham's louche magnetism; he seems to have been a bore and a drip who'd never inspire anyone to anything, let alone fire an artist's imagination. Waugh was never in love with him and neither was anyone else. Not that Hugh cared either way. When he fell over drunk in 1936, and hit his head and died, Waugh was in Abyssinia and heard about it from his parents in North London when he got back–they'd read it in the newspapers. Any subsequent claim of intimate friendship between the two men appears to be a projection backwards. Like Proust, Waugh created in his writings a milieu which was then superimposed on the real world of the past. What had in actuality been a number of scattered events, in which Waugh–and Proust–had often been marginal observers, became transformed in retrospect into a biographical drama of intense and conscious relationships. The various real-life characters were delighted to be co-opted into this mythologised pantheon–even dukes have to endure countless nothing days–and the authors gratifyingly transformed themselves into centres of the social universe.

In practice Waugh was far more interested in the lively Lygon sisters whom he now met for the first time and often visited until his second marriage a few years later–and he was never in love with any of them either. The set-up supplied Evelyn not only with friends but also with useful background. From 1931 on, his letters–and presumably his conversation–were full of casual remarks about estate maps, gun rooms and green baize doors, designed to convince the recipient of how thoroughly to the manor born he was (although he never deceived himself; one of the attractive aspects of Waugh is his ability to recognise his own pretentiousness at critical moments). Gentrification was not completed until 1937 when he married Laura Herbert in front of a very respectable guest list, bought Piers Court, and was granted a coat of arms. From 1937 can also be dated a rapid hardening of the exterior personality and a deepening of his unhappiness.

Waugh was a very physical man. His writing conveys an act of incision and sculptural pleasure. Probably he copulated with the same self-abusive gusto as he ate and drank. Before he'd finished with it he'd fathered six children. But clearly he was bisexual by temperament and loved to 'camp'—how those vivid check suits exploded off him! In the film *The Scarlet Woman*, made immediately after Oxford with several cronies from the Hypocrites Club, Waugh chose for himself the part of Sligger Urquhart, the homosexual Dean of Balliol, and then indulged in outrageously effeminate posturings on the screen, mincing about, sitting on boys' knees, hugging them, stroking their hair. To see this film to-day is to see a creature of almost Nijinskian levity, thoroughly uninhibited in his portrayal of pagan pleasures.

Eight years after his second marriage, Waugh's love for Alastair Graham would burst out afresh in the form of an intense nostalgia and he would make Alastair the hero/anti-hero not of his best novel but of the one closest to his private dreams. *Brideshead Revisited* lost intensity in its second half and I was going to suggest that it was because

Sebastian leaves the scene to be replaced by his rather bloodless sister Julia. That may be true, but loss of focus and vitality in the second half is a feature of every one of Waugh's novels except *Pinfold* (which is very short) and *Put Out More Flags* (for me his best book, with his earlier 'comic' and later 'serious' manner in ideal balance; also amazingly detached in the circumstances).

Not only does homosexual emotion resurface in *Brideshead*, the 'camp' does too. The monologues of Anthony Blanche are one of the book's star features. Wholly convincing as the outrageous prattle of a cultivated queen, they are extended way beyond their narrative functions because, quite simply, Waugh is having such a gorgeous time with them. But Waugh does something more profound with Blanche which it is possible to miss since it is disguised by comedy. He makes him the artistic conscience of the novel. At the end when the narrator, now a painter, is enjoying a successful show of his new work, Blanche unexpectedly turns up from abroad and exposes the pictures for what they are, 't-t-terrible t-t-tripe', the watery products of that English fear of causing offence. This is, as it were, Harold Acton flying in from the world of Picasso, Stravinsky and Diaghilev. So when it came to the crunch Waugh did not, in this novel at least, betray the values and demands of art in the interests of social acceptability – unlike, paradoxically, Harold Acton himself.

That was in art. In Waugh's life it was different. Ambivalence terrified him as though it were quicksand. The ruthless suppression of complex aspects of his character must have contributed to his general distemper and thereby to his addiction to drink and pills and to his bromide-induced nervous breakdown. In post-1937 conversation and letters he now refers to homosexuals as 'buggers', the straighthearty name for them in those days, ostentatiously crushing out all tenderness from the subject. But he can't deceive himself entirely. In *The Ordeal of Gilbert Pinfold* one of the first things the voices do is accuse Pinfold of being 'queer'. He goes into greater definition – not 'nancy' or 'pouf' but 'butch'. In his physical relationship with Graham, Waugh had seemingly been the more active partner.

In 1977 the *New Statesman* published a letter in which an American, Telford Gosling Spratt, announced that he was researching a book to be called *Evelyn Waugh: The Gay Years* and appealing for reminiscences. Nothing came of it and the title was hilarious, reminiscent of a Fred Astaire film. But it's definitely a topic. John Betjeman once exclaimed on the radio 'Oh, we were all queer then!' Waugh could never have been that carefree. The later rejection of so much of himself – of that generosity of spirit and enlarged capacity for life represented by his bisexuality – and his recourse to caricatured forms of religion and of social image, were disastrous. Existence became for him ever more loathsome, his days ever more alcoholic and miserable. Which would not be so objectionable had this state of affairs been of benefit to his art. But alas it was disastrous for that too. The books go terribly down hill. Whole tracts of them become nothing more than posey propaganda. The lightness went out of his work because it went out of his life.

The syndrome is not unique. The arc of the playwright John Osborne's life presents an unlikely parallel. An important attachment to another male early on, followed by professional success turning into drunken dandification, and to belligerent homophobic squirehood in the fourth phase. Both Osborne and Waugh presented a ludicrous spectacle in their last years, as if the 'camp' had to find an outlet somewhere and did so in theatrical plumage. Since both were astute observers of the human scene they must have recognised their absurdity and in part relished it. Which makes it 'ambivalence' or 'love-hate' by another route. To parody with such gross indecorum the squire role they had adopted was a form of offence against it, and what began as an awareness of the comedy of life became with the passing years a Dionysiac orgy of enraged mockery and despair. Both Osborne and Waugh had gay chums to the very end. Osborne incidentally was another one I missed; out of the blue he proposed a rendezvous with me at the Cadogan Hotel in Sloane Street, where Oscar Wilde was arrested, but I was in the South of France and couldn't make it. And Alastair Graham? From the range of photographs to hand one can see that he was never sartorially excessive in this way. Though usually smart, to the point of dapper, he was also – socially – the real thing: a reserved upper-class man.

What you are reading is a story of shame and hiding. If most of the hiding was Graham's, most of the shame was Waugh's. Waugh of course became an international celebrity, whereas Graham's life, subsequent to their relationship, entered a fog of obscurity and strangeness.

•

The years from 1934 to 1937 are particularly crucial to Graham. Up to that time he had travelled extensively in the Mediterranean. After it, he is a recluse. Why?

Giving up work, the loss of his gorgon-protectress mother, the desire to evade the ghosts of the past, these factors no doubt played their part. But could there have been a more urgent trigger? In 1936 (as I am to learn) he was staying with Clough Williams-Ellis at Portmeirion and heard that the Wern was for sale much further down the coast. That same year he bought it from a Major Evans and moved there in 1937. Living in the lodge were a gardener and his thirteen-year-old daughter Lottie and they stayed on. I decided to revisit New Quay.

I saw Lottie Evans, Graham's housekeeper, again in March 1990, this time in her council house on the edge of New Quay. She had retired.

'Can you remember Mr Graham's arrival at the Wern?'

'Oh yes. He came with Mrs Cooke the housekeeper and George Wood the butler who'd both been with his mother at Barford. Mrs Cooke had been in his family's service since Mr Graham was three years old and she trained me as a maid. Mr Graham did up the Wern beautifully. It's full of knick-knacks now, but when he had it, it was full of big oil paintings.'

Other local people were also more willing to fill in the gaps. The outbreak of the Second World War forced Graham to participate far more in local life and he developed several robust tastes: beer, sailing, fishing at sea. He went on a boat for the relief of Dunkirk, he joined the Royal Observer Corps, was for a time liaison officer with the US Navy, and also acquired a yacht, the Osprey.

Dylan Thomas was living in New Quay during the war and Graham didn't have a very high opinion of him and told a local reporter, Lyn Ebenezer, in 1978 (uncharitably given that it was the twenty-fifth anniversary of Thomas's death) that Dylan 'was quite boring in company, at least that's how I always found him, and he was forever begging for money.'

In 1945, as local press cuttings reveal, Graham had been involved in a shooting incident at Majoda, the bungalow occupied by Thomas and his wife Caitlin. They'd all been drinking at the Black Lion pub with a Captain Richard Killick who'd served in Greece. The man was married to a childhood friend of Dylan's called Vera and he became convinced that the poet had seduced his wife and had a threesome with Caitlin (which would have been in keeping). The party returned to Majoda and some time later the Captain followed, arrived outside and started firing at them through the keyhole. Then he burst in with a Sten gun and strafed the ceiling with bullets, shouting 'You're nothing but a bunch of egotists!'.

Graham told Richard Jones, whom he met in the early 1950s at an annual dinner of the New Quay Yacht Club, that Killick had thrown a hand grenade into Thomas's bungalow and that, fearful for the Thomas children asleep in the next room, Graham covered it with a cushion and gallantly sat upon it. But Killick wasn't that mad – later it was discovered he'd defused the grenade before tossing it in. Graham reportedly said that 'By speaking to the Captain and discussing the current situation in Greece, I managed either to make him interested or bored him sufficiently for him to calm down. He agreed to accompany me to his house, Ffynnon Feddyg, which was next door.'

When the case came up at Lampeter in midsummer, the Captain faced four charges, including one of attempting to murder Dylan Thomas. Graham, who was a witness for the prosecution, received a phonecall from his friend David Talbot Rice who by coincidence was the Captain's commanding officer and appearing for the defence.

Graham concluded 'We were all, including Dylan, very glad when the Captain was cleared by the jury. He was a gentleman, and I'm certain that it was the drink, and the fact that his war experiences had affected his nerves that made him act as he did.'

When Lyn Ebenezer asked Graham how he'd got to know the Dylan Thomases, he replied 'Through Augustus John who at the time was painting the portrait of a woman in Aberaeron. He called one night with Caitlin. They had one of the Thomas children with them who was placed in my bed while the rest of us had a few drinks. Suddenly Caitlin, who was an acknowledged dancer, stripped off and danced naked on the table. And when I fetched her child, the child had wet my bed.'

After the war, Graham's secretiveness and distaste for life beyond New Quay grew stronger. Dylan Thomas called him 'the thin-vowelled laird' in a letter to Margaret Taylor and used him as the model for Lord Cut-Glass in *Under Milk Wood* of 1954. 'Lord Cut-Glass lives in a house and a life at siege. Any minute or dark day now, the unknown enemy will loot and savage downhill, but they will not catch him napping'.

In 1958 Graham decided to sell Wern Newydd. Money was getting tight. Mrs Cooke had died and so had the butler George Wood. Servants of their calibre would never exist again. He had tried to find some, advertising for live-in help, recalled Lottie Evans. A couple arrived from

Swansea, stayed two nights and left, vexed by Graham's exacting standards – and the fact that the Wern still had no electricity or mains water. Inside it the atmosphere must have been pure Regency.

'Except,' said Lottie, 'an enormous paraffin burner in the kitchen! I told him I couldn't carry on working up there and doing it all. He had a big sale with a marquee on the lawn. But even though he sold so much, Rock Street was *full* of papers and books and furniture.'

'But why did he hide away here?'

Always the same question.

'Oh...I don't want to go into all that. Ask them up at the Wern. Have you been up to the Wern yet?'

No. And it was time that I did.

•

The Thomas family, no relations of the poet, purchased Wern Newydd from Alastair Graham and they kindly invited me over for a drink. In the nine years since I'd driven past it and been so taken by its lovely location, the surroundings had altered completely. A garish petrol station had been installed opposite, a holiday camp put up next door, and the Wern itself developed as a commercial riding stable. But I'd never been inside, and when I did it silenced me. It's a wonderful, romantic old place.

The present structure is mostly seventeenth century with parts dating back to the thirteenth. There is much panelling and a wide wooden staircase with shallow tread and barley sugar banisters. Henry Tudor, subsequently Henry VII, stayed here for a night in 1485 on his way to the Battle of Bosworth.

Mrs Thomas said 'When we took over, the grounds were in a terrible state. Alastair Graham couldn't have had anything done for years. So overgrown was it, that we didn't realise there was a stream running through the garden. But the house was beautiful inside. We found a number of his old books thrown out in the rain with the rubbish. What was so odd was that they were very personal books, the sort you'd think he'd want to hold on to.'

The Thomases retrieved them and put them back in the library where they currently reside, and they include Graham's mother's Prayer Book (Alistair has viciously scraped her bookplate out of it); a Book of Ballads inscribed to Alastair's father by his tutor at Eton; and two further Prayer Books both inscribed 'Alastair Graham from Mother, First Communion May 13th 1918'. Since Alastair's father did not die until 1921 it is curious that the inscriptions are only from the mother – and so very cold. Forty years later the son threw them into the bin. They meant nothing. Or too much, and he wanted to leave all that behind. Either way, he'd obviously ditched the roaring Catholicism mentioned by Claud Cockburn.

'We also found a bill,' said Dr Thomas (who is a ship's surgeon). 'When Graham first came to the Wern he devoted most of his energy to doing it up. The bill says he spent £5,000 on renovations which was an enormous sum before the Second World War – and it can't have been the only bill. He was famous for his parties, in the earlier period anyway. Caitlin Thomas danced naked on the dining-table [again!]. Viscount Tredegar was a good friend. Tom Herbert, the local vet, was a close friend of Alastair's, and he told us that Edward VIII visited Graham at the Wern incognito.'

Tom Herbert had been one of my original sources. I was told he knew a lot. But he'd said virtually nothing while Graham was alive. And now it was too late. Herbert died several weeks before my current visit to New Quay.

'When we arrived,' said Mrs Thomas, 'the pine panelling in the dining-room was painted pink. He'd also converted the musicians' hall into a chapel and painted it green and had Mass said in the house.'

There had been a vogue between the wars for painting wood panelling in unnatural colours. Ottoline Morrell had started it at Garsington when she did it up in 1915, breaking with tradition and painting the rooms of Elizabethan oak in grey, green, scarlet and canary-yellow.

Graham had become a Roman Catholic as early as September 13th 1924 but Lottie Evans recalls no religious goings-on at the Wern. 'Very lapsed, I'd say,' was her remark when I put it to her. Jan Orpen however, a local drinking pal of Graham's, remembers that 'A Father Bathbrick used to call at the Wern from time to time to keep him in touch. Bathbrick was a famous drinker but Graham, at least when I knew him, was quite moderate. He could have an evil temper and was very self-centred, but he could mix with anyone and never talked down. After he moved to Rock Street he never saw anyone of his own level. He was a very good cook by the way. I've got a little pamphlet he prepared, *20 Different Ways of Cooking New Quay Mackerel*.'

I asked Dr Thomas why he thought Graham had escaped to this place in the 1930s.

'I don't think he had any choice. He was told by the police – go to ground or go to prison. You know he was part of a homosexual ring in London which was very illegal in those days. There must have been some sort of crackdown in the offing. Rosa Lewis too advised him to get the hell out of town. I gather he was briefly recalled to London during the Suez Crisis because of his knowledge of Egypt.'

So here at last was something more specific about Graham's disappearing act. Tom Herbert told me that Graham had said to him 'Rosa Lewis was very unkind to me.' Could this have been what he meant? I'd heard that Graham was quite close to Rosa Lewis, the 'Duchess of Duke Street', friend of Edward VII and patronne of the Cavendish Hotel. This was – somehow – through his mother's only brother, the deceased William Low, who came to England at the end of the nineteenth century with £750,000 and proceeded to spend it. Willie Low died in 1905 but Rosa never forgot a spender. In the company of Graham, Waugh had visited the Cavendish Hotel. Rosa Lewis becomes 'Lottie Crump' in one of the most brilliant scenes in *Vile Bodies*. She was outraged and never forgave Waugh, and Graham must have taken the flak.

At Rock Street, Graham went out less and less often, apart from his regular drink at the Dolau Inn. Lottie Evans said 'When he moved into the town he told me he would be spending his winters abroad from now on but he only spent about three nights away from the house the whole time he was there.'

'We tried to invite him to dinner once,' said Mrs Thomas, 'but his reply was "I can't, I'm not fit to be seen".'

That terrible expression again.

Though Graham became president of the New Quay branch of the local Lifeboat Association and was accepted by many of the townsfolk, something sinister and unexplained always clung to him. When I first met him in that pub in 1979 my overriding impression was of pathos, notwithstanding his little joke about Waugh's endowment. Much of Graham's delicate camouflage was blown away at the end of his life when *Brideshead Revisited* was broadcast on television. Graham didn't have a television set himself and a local doctor, Dr Vasey, collected him in the car to watch it at the Vasey household. He loved the show initially, until it became more widely known that he was the original of its pivotal character and the press descended – but they had no more luck than I did. Life in New Quay had been possible because his homosexuality was an unspoken thing. Now here it was on national television, not in your face exactly – Sturridge didn't force the sex angle – but beyond inuendo.

Lottie remembered that 'It made him very unhappy. The telephone hardly rang before, and now it didn't stop ringing. At one point he was frightened to leave the house.' Oh dear, my own guilt rankled…But then I thought, for God's sake, what a misery Graham was, for apart from Flyte's squalid end, the association was astoundingly flattering! And yet how perceptive Waugh had been in the book: the curse of Sebastian Flyte is his failure of nerve in the face of life's demands and opportunities.

Taking me into the front room of her council house, Lottie pointed to an Edwardian genre pastel in an oval gilt frame. It was of a boy with golden curls and blue eyes wearing a large straw hat.

'That's Mr Graham when he was nine. I always loved it and his niece in South Africa gave it to me.'

It would have been done immediately before the First World War and was highly evocative of that lost paradise. Yet once again I heard some of Anthony Blanche's words from the novel: 'You mustn't blame Sebastian if at times he seems a little insipid…When I hear him talk I am reminded of that in some ways nauseating picture of "Bubbles"'.

But that wasn't the important thing. What was important was that I had a new lead.

'Did you say Alastair Graham had a niece?'

'Yes. Two of them. Sybil's daughters.'

'Did they find any letters?'

'I don't know. The African niece, Mrs Davidson, got everything and cleared the house – you should ask her.'

'Do you have the nieces' telephone numbers?'

Lottie did and she gave me both.

Firstly I rang Graham's younger niece in Scotland, Mrs Kitty Macduff Duncan. 'I'm not going to co-operate,' she said. 'You're going to drag up all that nasty business, I know.'

What nasty business? This threw me and I went off at a tangent and rang the head of the family, Sir Charles Graham of Netherby who couldn't have been nicer but who could only remember that Alastair Graham 'wrote to me when I was engaged in 1944 and sent me a wedding present, purely as a cousin, but he didn't come to the wedding. His father Hugh was my grandfather's brother and I remember hearing as a boy that Hugh was a wonderful shot.'

'Did you know that Alastair Graham was the model for Sebastian Flyte?'

'Well, I never heard that! I'd no idea. I'm absolutely

fascinated – and I know all about *Brideshead* because I was a great friend of George Howard and they filmed it at Castle Howard. Do you know what became of Alastair?'

'He died about eight years ago.'

'Did he. Did he.'

Finally, with very little optimism, I rang the other niece, Mrs Jane Davidson, in Pretoria. The phone was picked up almost at once. 'You're jolly lucky to get me,' she said, sounding a great deal closer than she was.

'Am I? Why?'

'Because people almost never get me.'

This could have been Lady Circumference speaking to me on a sunny day, open, confident, affable, in a very English way. Forty-five minutes later she was still talking and bubbling over with the sheer pleasure of entering family history.

'Oh, I remember Evelyn very well! He was awfully nice – very quiet but amusing. I only saw him when I came to England on holidays from Kenya where we lived but he used to lift me up through the skylight at Barford, which was that dome which you saw, and we'd go out on to the roof together where there was a marvellous view of the garden and the Greek temple which was the garden's main feature. Mrs G made a goldfish pond – Evelyn helped her build it – in front of the temple and they put a statue of Mercury in it like they have at Christ Church in Oxford.'

'So they got on then?'

'Who got on?'

'Evelyn and Alastair's mother.'

'Oh, Evelyn was far better with Mrs G than Alastair was! Evelyn used to take the dogs for long walks and practically lived there at times, even when Alastair was away, and used to write in an awful bare little attic room with a tailor's dummy in it and that skylight above because there were no windows. Mrs G – Jessie Graham – she dominated Ali with his artistic nature which she didn't understand. She hunted, gardened furiously, and thought nothing of cycling forty miles. She cycled all round France. When Evelyn married the other Evelyn they went to stay with Mrs G and there's a line in her diary for 1928 which says "the 2 Evelyns played about in the garden" as if they were puppies. And there's an interesting passage on Greece for the same year – Mrs G went to stay with Ali in Athens. But her writing is terribly difficult to read. Her father was a cotton merchant, you know, in Savannah and his mansion is now open to the public. Thackeray stayed there in Savannah with him and wrote *The Virginians* in one of the bedrooms. But Jessie was brought up a good deal in England and Evelyn I'm sure didn't really think of her as other than English.

'You see, Jessie's father was widowed twice. Her elder stepsister Amy married into the Grenfell family and when Jessie's mother died she was sent to England to live with Amy Grenfell and one of this huge clan was Sir Francis Grenfell who was Sirdar of Egypt and afterwards Governor of Malta and Gozo – '

'What's a Sirdar exactly?'

'I think it's sort of head of the army out there and so of course this led to a family connection with that part of the world long before Ali was born. A stream of people went out to stay with Sir Francis, and Jessie and Hugh spent their honeymoon on the Nile, probably on the Sirdar's yacht. Her brother William was Andrew Low's only son and did quite well out of it. Willie Low transferred to England and lived only a few miles from Barford and he was also part of the Marlborough House set. He was a racing man, mad on shooting, and knew Edward VII, and then you see Rosa Lewis had been Uncle Willie's kitchen maid at one time and Rosa learnt a lot about southern cooking from Willie's negress cook Mosianna.'

'So that's how Alastair and Evelyn came to link up with Rosa Lewis?'

'Yes, it was a very natural connection and Ali sometimes lived at the Cavendish Hotel when he was in London. But he hated horses and shooting which is why he sold Barford although it was a white elephant, he couldn't sell it for years.'

'So when his mother died, he tried to sell Barford House but couldn't, he was stuck with it?'

'That's right. He certainly didn't want to live there, with all the memories, and all the locals who'd known Jessie and Willie; they were breathing down Ali's neck because he wasn't married and always wanting him to dance with their daughters which wasn't his thing at all.'

'Alastair not liking shooting and horses would presumably suit Evelyn.'

'Evelyn hadn't a clue about that sort of thing and wasn't interested either, being artistic like Ali.'

'Ali's artistic nature, that's also why he wandered round the Levant.'

'Of course it was, yes, but his diplomatic appointment was through Louise Loraine, Sir Percy's wife, who was related to the Grahams via the American connection.

Sorry, this all gets a bit complicated but it's interesting the way everything connects up and it's a world gone by. Ali's job was to look after Sir Percy's entertaining and Ali loved that. When Ali was in Cairo he had to take Mussolini's daughter round the Pyramids, that sort of thing. But he first went to Egypt with Mrs G at the age of eighteen before he went to university and at Port Said he ran away, just like that, ran off into the town, and Jessie had to return to England without him. How he was discovered again I don't know but people said it was nothing new. People often remarked that Ali had a habit of disappearing! He then travelled a great deal in that part of the world *before* his diplomatic engagement. I found letters to someone called Claud dated 1926, 1927.'

'That would be Claud Cockburn.'

'Do you think so? Who was Claud Cockburn? Except for one written in Crete, they're typed copies. I don't know why Ali kept them. He didn't keep much else of a personal nature. I can send them if you like.'

Clearly Alastair had left everything to the right niece.

One week later a thick envelope arrived on my doormat, covered with bright African stamps. It contained photocopies of five letters from Graham to Cockburn, a letter from Robert Byron to Graham, various other material, and a covering letter of sixteen foolscap pages from Mrs Davidson herself supplying many further biographical points. It was as if she hoped, after years of maddening and largely pointless secrecy over her uncle, the record might now be made clear.

Are you getting accustomed to the spiral structure of this piece, how I acquired my information in a roundabout way? It doesn't matter whether or not you're able to hold all the details in your head as we go along – I've checked backwards to ensure that everything does cohere properly. But I hope I'm conveying a progressive revelation, as a painter starting with a few lines scattered about the canvas will eventually end up with a portrait as complete as he can make it.

Here are some of the many things Graham's African niece put in her long letter to me. General Robert E. Lee had been Jessie Low's godfather. Jessie and Hugh Graham rented houses until they moved to Barford in 1917, the first property they owned. Alastair was a timid child, frightened of cows. He went to a day school in Leamington Spa and was at Wellington College a very short time and left at fifteen. Mrs Davidson thought he must have refused to go back. He lasted only a short time at Oxford too, but went back to the University for the Railway Club dinner, November 28th 1923, on the Penzance to Aberdeen service. Mrs Davidson enclosed a photocopy of the menu, signed by 'Harold Acton', 'Peter Quennell' and other fellow travellers. I notice that Waugh is the only one who signs it simply with his Christian name, at a time when undergraduates, continuing the example set at school, customarily called each other by their surname plain.

Alastair's letters to Claud Cockburn are vivacious but straightforward accounts of the delights and pains of travel in that era. Here follow some extracts. His companion in the first is a man called Benvenuto who Mrs Davidson said was not Italian, so goodness knows what he was.

12th February 1926　　　　　Kairouan, Barbary

Dear Claud,

We left Tunis yesterday so early in the morning.
I was all scrumpled up with sleep, and it was pouring with rain...From Sousse the train goes inland...
the country gets more and more desolate...And
then we saw Kairouan suddenly quite close. It is all
surrounded by ramparts so that you cannot see any
houses. The ramparts have little towers here and
there and are crenelated with vast white teeth on
top, so that the city grins at you.

We are staying in the Hotel de France...Sev-
eral men spoke to us and admired Benvenuto's
rings and shewed us their finger rings also. One
rather fat man with a very smart embroidered
coat asked us to a party. We hurried over our
dinner and met him under the old gateway. He
led us through the dark and sinister streets to a
ramshackle but brightly lit house where lots of
draped men were lying about on the floor drinking coffee and smoking strange pipes. Several
of them bowed and made oriental gestures as
we came in and gave us coffee to drink. Soon
one man began to beat a drum and to sing
a dull and discordant chant. A youth got up
and stood on an alfa-grass mat. He had a little bag-
pipe in his hand and a great many coloured silks
tied round his stomach. He danced a rather
obscene and suggestive dance, rolling his belly and
buttocks, accentuated by the silks...The old men

loved the dance. They applauded furiously and threw kisses to the youth.

Then the proprietor brought us a silver and ebony pipe to smoke. There was a little boy sitting on the floor grinding herbs to powder on a wooden board. This they put into the pipe for us to smoke. It is called kif, and they explained that as alcohol was forbidden them, they used kif to excite their brains and bodies. It has a pungent odour, burns the tongue and gives one rather a headache but is otherwise pleasant enough. Several others smoked the pipe with us and I was frightened of catching diseases because some of them had sores on their lips.

...An old man was sitting next to me with a wicker basket in his hands, and when the dance was over he opened the basket which was full of serpents, and they slid out all over the floor; but he took a clarinet and made them dance to him and when they had finished fed them on eggs.

May (?) 1926   4 Odos Mantzarou,
                                                Athens.

Dear Claud,

I am sitting in a deck-chair in a kind of area or hole in the garden, under the honeysuckle bush because three women are helping Niko to faire the chambre propre...

...I have had nothing to eat for a week except a sheep which we bought and kept in the bathroom and sacrificed by the Ilissus on Saturday in accordance with the Orthodox rite.

...All Niko's friends come from Constantinople and consequently all my employees come from there. They hate Athens and say how lovely is Constantinople; and then they begin to weep because never again will they be able to go back there. It is all so sad...All things in Greece happen like this. Most of them are mad and the rest are homosexual nymphomaniacs, but they all have a certain amount of charm.

June 16th 1927   Canea,
                                                  Crete.

Dear Claud and Benvenuto,

I am so sorry I have not written to you for so long. I have been staying here in this delightful island, which floats curiously undecided as to which continent should embrace it. It may any day swim and attach itself to the shores of Africa, Asia or Europe.

The earthquakes here are so delightful. They have them almost twice a week. Strange rumblings from the bowels of the ground, dark scented winds rush up from beneath the earth; the trees quiver and the bells in the church steeples tinkle unsteadily, while stones fall from the mountain tops.

Yesterday I came down from the high mountains where I have been living. For a week I have slept in caves or by the fires of shepherds...

Why do you not leave the Gothic climate and leafy beer gardens of Germany and come for only a little while to the south?

This last, undated, is the letter in manuscript (Graham's hand is upright, loopy and legible), so presumably it was never posted or Alastair made a fair copy. Benvenuto seems to have decamped to Germany with Cockburn for some reason. Mrs Davidson also had two letters from the Loraines begging Alastair to go to Ankara with them but he refused, though he did briefly visit them there and found the place depressing – wolves came out at night and raided the dustbins.

Some weeks later a second gaudy envelope arrived from South Africa containing a stack of photographs and another long letter from Jane Davidson. The photographs included a number of Graham out and about New Quay and the Middle East, and also several of his mother Jessie, no beauty but looking natural, unfussy and compact in Edwardian dress. The most important was a close-up of Graham at the age of eighteen, on the eve of going up to Oxford. Soft wavy hair brushed to one side, a spotless complexion, and wonderfully serious eyes. The mouth is wide and well shaped but the lips are thin – a hint of the peevishness which would see the corners of the mouth turn down in later years. The weakest feature is the nose, somewhat fleshy. Not film star looks but an English sweetness and vulnerability you could definitely fall for.

Mrs Davidson wrote: 'Mrs G kept him short of cash and he always travelled 2nd class. Rosa Lewis used to make up hampers for him to take away with him. In 1925 he came out to visit us in Kenya and my mother wrote to an American aunt that "Ali seemed completely uninterested in everything and never made any comments about the country but he got on well with his riding." Which was news to me. I thought he only rode camels – he loved camels, told me so. I found a letter from the Jesuit Father Martindale sent to Ali in Kenya saying he was worried about having let him join the R.C. church as he felt that really it was only Ali's artistic nature which had attracted him to it. He also said he was worried about the people Ali associated with at Oxford!! + warned him – too late!! rather amusing since these people were nearly all Catholics!!!'

In the summer of 1924 Evelyn and Alistair were at Barford planning a walking tour to Ireland. 'Typically they passed the hat round – and got £10!! Ali and Sybil used to bait their mother + were *rude all the time*. I enjoyed staying there alone with her and so did Evelyn. Evelyn noticed that the service was not so good when Jessie was away and Ali was in charge, but she was keen on press-ganging the boys to help in the garden sweeping up leaves etc., which is why they were always hiding from her. She took amazing risks – quite frightening!! She climbed 24 foot expansion-ladder at Barford cutting down the ivy on the Clock Tower with BOTH HANDS FREE!! AGED 70. I SAW THIS MYSELF!!!'

It does something to exonerate Alastair's awkwardness that Mrs Davidson should mention that her mother, Graham's sister Sybil, also had problems with Jessie. Joan Davidson related next an incident which throws much light on Waugh's sudden severance from the Graham household.

For Alastair's 21st in 1925 Mrs Graham had, with typical ardour, built a large extra room on to the house. Equally typically the projected ball never took place, but afterwards on a long stool in this room there always reposed the king-sized *Times Atlas of the World*, the idea being that it would always be available for easy consultation. But in 1931, after leaving Malvern and his riding lessons with Jack Hance (he was determined to fill the gaps in his social equipment), Waugh stayed at Barford alone with Mrs Graham and ripped out a whole page from this atlas to use on his upcoming African trip. Since she consulted the atlas a great deal herself, she noticed at once and was so outraged by his vandalism that Waugh was banished for ever from her house and from her society. It was such a violent thing for him to have done that he must have been prepared for the worst. His ruthlessness was deliberate desecration.

Jane Davidson ended her second letter with 'Hope this info into Alastair's life some use – they were an amusing crowd. Of course all the CASH EVAPORATED *very quickly*!! Willy left practically everything to his mistress!!'

Christopher Hollis was, like many others, surprised by how complete was the break between Graham and Waugh. In his book *Oxford in the Twenties* Hollis wrote... 'in general Evelyn was more faithful than anyone whom I ever knew to his old friends and always welcomed them gladly to the end of his life, but Alastair Graham, who was the closest of all his friends, passed completely out of his life'. Hollis overlooks the difficulties in Graham's personality; Waugh was not less difficult but more gregariously so. And their relationship had been an affair, not straightforward friendship, and when affairs end some unease or rancour can enter in.

When my correspondence with Mrs Davidson resumed by telephone I wanted to be quite sure there were no misunderstandings and asked 'Can I use this material in my piece?'

'Of course! That's why I'm giving it to you!' A clutch of exclamation marks sprouted in the air. She obviously loved her uncle very much, but she loved the real one, not the pretend one.

'Why do you think his friendship with Waugh ended so completely?' I asked.

'Well, Evelyn was a terrible social climber – and he got worse. After his first marriage broke up he got awfully grand. The thing was he came from a low church, almost Baptist background, you know, that class, and I think he had a chip on his shoulder. I once asked Ali "Why aren't you friends with Evelyn any more?" and Ali said "Oh, you know, Evelyn became such a bore, such a snob".'

'Yes, someone told me Alastair wasn't snobbish.'

'That's right – he was a very good mixer. He loved the pub in New Quay and the people there.'

'One can't imagine Waugh being able to chat up the locals. Among Alastair's papers, was there anything from Waugh?'

'I was surprised to find nothing. Alastair kept nothing from Evelyn.'

'And why do you think he became so withdrawn as a person?'

'Ali got Barford and its contents but my mother – Ali's sister – got most of the money. So really he couldn't afford to keep up the social round. Nancy Mitford stayed at the Wern – she was the cousin of his friend Mark Ogilvie-Grant. And Gerry Wellington stayed there. But Evelyn never attempted to visit.'

'You know what I mean. He didn't take up with any-one else.'

'Then in middle age he...didn't suffer fools gladly.'

'But after Waugh, Alastair is not associated with anyone romantically. Was he lonely?'

'Perhaps he wanted to be. Alastair never knew what boredom meant. He preferred to read all day. History mostly. He used to go out trawling–he was friends with a trawler captain–and lobster fishing. Whenever you went to see him you always got lobster–and toadstools, the sort you can eat, he was very keen on those. And he liked to do needlepoint, petit point, to pass the weeks which sounds rather cissy but he needlepointed all the dining-room chairs beautifully with lobsters and crabs and pink seaweed. But it ruins the eyes, you know, and he had to give it up.'

'Not a very happy life.'

'Well, actually...Alastair's was not a very happy death.'

'Would you tell me?'

He'd been ill for some time. With no one else in the house he was obliged to enter an old people's home up the coast at Aberaeron. He hated it. 'And some awful woman got into his bed. That really upset him. He went to have a bath and when he got back he found this completely mental woman occupying his bed.'

Alastair rallied slightly from his illness and decided to return to Rock Street but soon after getting home he started to cough up blood. The doctors thought it might be tuberculosis and he was taken to the chest hospital at Machynlleth. In fact he didn't have TB. He died in

Machynlleth Hospital in October 1982 from cancer of the pancreas. There were no obituaries, there was no burial, there is no gravestone. His ashes were scattered on the sea from a lifeboat off New Quay and he was finally able to do what he so often wanted to do, to disappear from the world without memorial or trace.

Yet the reason for this self-sequestration in a place far from his previous existence, that question still tugs. Anthony Powell said 'I think he was just like that. I always found him sort of buttoned-up, an odd figure, awfully difficult to talk to.' Others have claimed the threat of homosexual scandal, and certainly British law at the time could employ state terror against homosexuals if it chose; when one is tempted to dream of 'the good old days' it is well to remember that in the United Kingdom they were often splenetic, soot-covered, and primly cruel. At the age of thirty-three Alastair retreated to New Quay, as remote as anywhere on mainland Britain, and hardly left the place again. Sir Charles Graham also told me that Wales is the only part of the United Kingdom where the Graham family has no blood connections whatsoever.

But finally one of my contacts, Jack Patrick Evans, said something very pregnant when I visited him in his nursing-home one windswept afternoon. Two things actually – the first was 'Our paths crossed while Graham was still at Oxford.' It is clear now that Evans knew a great deal about Graham's private life and that they'd slept together, but he never gave on that score. The second thing he said was 'Yes, he was warned out of London by the police. Yes, there was the threat of prison. But it had nothing to do with homosexuality. What it had to do with was – there was a furore over a piece of jewelry.'

What on earth was that supposed to mean? Jack Patrick refused to be drawn further but was adamant that it was so – though added that he knew few of the details. Then he died. I have not been able to develop this lead in any way but I record it for a simple reason: it allows Alastair Graham to keep his mystery still.

Looking over this material one last time, it occurs to me that when at my first meeting with Alastair in the pub he said of Waugh that 'he wasn't well endowed in the other sense', I could well in my vulgar way have jumped to the wrong conclusion. Perhaps Graham was simply saying that Evelyn was poor, had no money, and Graham was remembering the onetime dearest and then ungrateful friend who had cadged off him, whose overdraft Alastair had guaranteed, and who had ended up bellowing drunkenly in White's club about buggers and pansies. Waugh bellowed thus in a desperate attempt 'to belong'. But Waugh never belonged: he was a misfit too – and he knew it.

•

It was the summer of 2007. I was working on a novel, a ghost story, one which is a fictional companion to this book, in that the novel also concerns itself with the disquieting state in which someone is neither present in one's life nor absent from it, and explores the abyss which can open up between someone or something *being there* and *not being there*. One place I didn't want to be was central London in July, so I was delighted when the authoress Susan Hill said

I could rent the flat in her barn while the regular tenant was in the Far East. Susan and her husband owned a stone farmhouse near Chipping Campden in the Cotswolds and she said that the opposite end of the barn was currently occupied by a family of owls. It sounded idyllic – and was. It was also a bit strange. Susan, across the lawn and immured in an upstairs room in front of a computer, herself occupied an interzone between being there and not being there; for throughout my four-week residency in her barn I was never invited to break bread under her roof. I tried to take her out to lunch – but she fended me off. This perplexed me, because Susan and I got on very well otherwise. It also set up a kind of tension of civility inside me; I felt an obligation to breach the invisible wall and so invited her and her husband Stanley to eat with me in the barn the evening before I left, in effect entertaining them on their own property.

But not long after my arrival there was a bigger drama, one heralded by a violent thunderstorm at dusk. Cloudbursts crashed over the hills and pink-hued lightning flashed on the walls of my sitting-room. The room was large, its walls white, and it had windows on three sides, so the experience of the storm was Wagnerian.

The next morning it was still raining. I looked out of the window with my mug of breakfast tea. Heavy flat rain. And Susan's drive was a yellow torrent. The back drive round the barn was another yellow torrent. Where the two linked up, in the direction of the road, there was deep flooding, while the ground floor of the barn itself was under several inches of water. We were marooned. And the rain continued. Susan rang the flat to make sure I was OK. By the end of the afternoon, water was pouring directly off the hills and this region of England was undergoing the worst flood in living memory.

All of which is to set the scene for...Barford. Later in the week, when the drive had drained a little and we could get in and out again, I hit the road in the car. To breathe. Thought I'd head up to Warwick and take a look at the castle. I found myself flying past Barford village on a shiny new by-pass with a trading estate recently put up. But the River Avon had burst its banks and Barford was on the far side of a silver sheet of floodwater half a mile across. It looked like the Isle of the Dead. The bypass fed me on to a massive and confusing motorway interchange but I kept my head and doubled back and was soon flying past Barford in the opposite direction. There must be a way to reach it, I thought. I saw temporary yellow signs, directing me onto this new speedway, that new speedway, past half-built housing developments, new factories springing up, and everywhere immense silver sheets of floodwater, and the signs to Barford always pointing to the far side of them. Suddenly the road coiled round on itself–I don't know how it happened–and I was driving over an ancient stone bridge up to its neck in water and into a settlement for human beings, with delightful red-brick cottages, and there along on the left was, yes, it was still stubbornly there, Barford House.

I pulled over beside the brick wall which shielded its front garden. A mass of dull modern houses had been built opposite. The wall was tipping backwards and the garden was now an overgrown jungle which entirely obscured the house from the road. The main gate had gone but an inner gate was just about holding together, its wooden palings snapped off and unpainted. There were three cars parked in the turning space but the house itself was shut-up, dead, rotting. Its once smart white was almost all washed off, exposing the brownish plaster beneath, unpainted since my previous visit decades before. But the six Ionic pilasters still looked sturdy – the central four rounded and the ones on either end squared off – with the dome intact above. The conservatory, attached to the left side, was green with mould and collapsing. I drove down a side road to view the back of the place, but couldn't get close because of another new housing development, but I did see that the walled garden had been severed from the main property and turned into public allotments. The drone of traffic from the motorway was low and incessant, contrasting eerily with the dereliction of the site. In this district of bright new prospects Barford House was the only abandoned thing, yet from its tangled, ruinous grounds there rose an immense variety of birdsong...

I sat in the car for absolutely ages, unable to move on, held by an intriguing spell; and now writing this, I return completely to that moment, to that mood of mystery and fretful discontent outside the gates of Barford House, with its protective garden wall on the very point of falling inwards. What was I waiting for? A voice from the past? The final collapse? No. I was luxuriating in melancholy. And the experience had something metaphysical about it and puts me in mind of a wonderful remark of Vasily Rozanov's...'All religions will pass away,' he wrote, 'but this will remain: sitting in a chair and looking into the distance.'

CHAPTER FIVE

Beyond the Blue Horizon

t had been the hottest August on record. The last day of the month came, a Sunday, and there was a good promenade concert that night at the Royal Albert Hall – Sibelius, Britten, Stravinsky. But I'd miss it since I'd promised to drive down to Sussex on the Sunday afternoon in order to help my friend Elisa whose mother had recently been transferred to a nursing home. Elisa had to go through the house prior to its sale, sorting out room after room of possessions, and she was dreading it. I got up at around 9 am, made a pot of tea, and switched on the box. Princess Diana had been killed in a car crash. Reports were only just coming through from Paris and the matter was still very confused.

Sometimes you find yourself doing things without having decided to do them, as though your conduct were being guided. Falling in love can be like this: you are swept up with someone and taken by events without consciously willing any of it. So on this morning I discovered I simply couldn't stay indoors in the flat, and at around 10.30 I found myself walking along Notting Hill Gate, holding a potted white cyclamen. Nobody had told me to do this. I hadn't even told myself to do it. And I'd never have guessed I would be doing it. In retrospect it's a great surprise to me that I did, because nothing in my life had been directly concerned with the Princess of Wales. But I was doing it. And I wasn't alone. There was a trickle of us on that strange Sunday morning, drifting through the flowery, stucco streets of Notting Hill towards Kensington Gardens, mostly single people, several couples, quite a few black women. And it was unusually quiet, as though somehow the streets were padded.

Suddenly the cyclamen felt heavy. I don't actually recall having bought it, or where I bought it, but I do remember being repelled by the cyclamens that were red and knowing that white, on this occasion, was the only and proper colour. There was an Arab café on Wellington Terrace called Café Diana which I'd never noticed before, or rather, I'd noticed a café but hadn't bothered to register what its name was, despite having walked past it hundreds of times. This morning was different. The café's owner had already set up a little memorial on the pavement, comprising a photograph of the Princess and a bouquet. I asked him about the origin of the name of his establishment and he told me they'd adopted it two years previously because Diana had often taken her boys there after collecting them from their day-school in Pembridge Square round the corner. I decided to put my cyclamen down at this impromptu site outside the café and continue onward to Kensington Palace to pay my respects.

Why Kensington Palace? Because, I suppose, it had been her home. But this wasn't something one was conscious of assessing. It was simply the only and obvious place to go. In the Broad Walk it was again apparent that others agreed with me. From all directions people were moving towards the Palace, not many, perhaps a hundred in all, but, viewed from the vantage of the north slope of the park, one could see how the Palace was exerting an irresistible, magnetic pull. Nobody was walking in any other direction. And it was all taking place silently.

At the great gilded gates facing south, people had begun to leave flowers. A dozen or so bunches were propped against them, some attached to the wrought iron scrolls. There were a couple of badly painted portraits of the Princess, seemingly the work of children, and a red satin heart with *Diana, we love you* on it. Obviously people were bringing personal items. A shrine seemed to be in the offing. Eventually a group of tourists arrived and began taking photographs but another mood took hold of them, their cameras halted and the tourists just stood there. I shifted about, vaguely nonplussed. Nobody spoke much, but there was unselfconscious eye contact and *no barriers between people*. If anyone said anything it was not in a whisper but in a quiet voice and was usually something like 'I can't believe it...' Goodness knows how long I remained there. The atmosphere was enthralling.

When I got back to the flat, my brother Peter rang. He too had been affected by the news and said he found himself unable to settle or do anything. 'It's like when John Lennon was murdered,' he said. 'She was the star of the nation. We've got no one like that now.' But for me the Lennon comparison wasn't enough. I thought also of President Kennedy and the suicide of Marilyn Monroe. They weren't enough either. Leaving the Ritz in Paris with a lover and – bang! The most legendary personality of the age had made the most astonishing exit. But later that day I continued as planned and drove down to Sussex to help Elisa sort out her mother's house, pointing at objects, putting stickers on some of them, relegating others – it was fascinating and objective, with that thank-God-not-me pleasure one has when taking someone else to the dentist.

Inside a coffin Princess Diana duly returned from France, coming in at Northolt aerodrome northwest of London. She disembarked to the sound only of a wind blowing across the runway. You will be able to hear this wonderful wind on the film. There was bound to be a film. They were recording everything. Meanwhile the pilgrimage of the people to Kensington Palace had swelled to unimaginable proportions. The Queen and the Royal family held themselves aloof from the rising flood, trying to outgrand popular sentiment. But the only effect of this was that they began to look smaller and smaller. Their stultification became embarrassing, pitiful, scandalous. The Queen throughout her entire reign had never looked so cheap, and when public feeling began to spill over into outrage, Her Majesty was forced to bring down to half-mast the Royal Standard which until then had been flying at full pitch over Buckingham Palace. There had been explanations of why the Royal Standard did this; how it could only be this-or-thatted for such and such an occasion: none of it washed. The callous statement atop the palace had to learn its simple, humane lesson – and learn it it did. Down came the standard to half-mast and the nation sighed with collective relief.

It would be several months before the Queen's stoicism found its admirers; compassion, sensitivity and self-revelation are warm human qualities; but for life one needs toughness too. And in later life nothing so becomes one as stoicism. The Queen's endurance in the face of the endless daily round, of her children's ineptitudes, of the crude insults and constant sniping, of terrorist death threats and the betrayal of servants and the intense public pressure to invade her most private space and very soul, is a story for someone else on another occasion, but one does wonder – was this her most vulnerable moment?

At a party to launch a literary gazetteer of Russia, done by Anna Benn and Rosamund Bartlett, the male intellectuals were putting forth a sneery attitude to the mourning of Princess Diana, including, to my surprise, Anna's editor Peter Straus. They spoke of 'mass hysteria' and 'fascistic mobs'. English intellectuals are generally of a puritan cast and puritanism is a post-Shakespearean development in English society. The intellectuals feared being castrated by participation in popular feeling, and cynicism was their weapon against it–but the impression they gave was of being dead at their core. For what was so striking about the public mourning of Diana was its dignity. Rather more hysterical indeed was the chatter of the intellectuals, and it is faintly alarming that such people are unable to distinguish between acts of mourning and acts of political fascism. As for cynicism and stoicism, they are not the same; in the classical world they were opposing philosophies, I believe. It is true that sometimes a nausea can arise at an excess of emotion and even I, at the literary party, asked 'Do you remember the previous Princess Diana?' 'No. Who was that?' 'Julie Christie in *Darling*.' Diana jokes appeared very quickly. What's the difference between a Skoda and a Mercedes? Diana wouldn't be seen seen dead in a Skoda. And far behind her, way off in the distance, hardly discernible, was another ghost, that of her Egyptian lover who died with her. Soon the conspiracy theorists would go into action. It would get nasty.

Regardless of one's particular reaction to the event, nobody was without a reaction. For the time being Diana's death abolished solitariness and we all lived in a village, everyone pushed out of the centre of their own existence by it. Yet among the heaps of nonsense which have followed in the years since, the question which has never been answered, and indeed not often asked, is *why* was there this bewildering and unprecedented reaction to her death? All the answers to the question so far have been too partial, too concerned with advancing an angled view. Nobody has quite nailed it. I don't mean the crash itself. We've nailed that. Of course it was an accident. This has been demonstrated over and over again in numerous court cases and public enquiries. What we haven't nailed is our response to it. Nobody has come up with a satisfactory explanation which marries human psychology to history, and this, presumably, is why the subject doesn't quite go away. The event may be fading into history but not that question, and its psychological aspect might begin with an analysis of this factor: the importance of being bewildered. Mystification is absolutely essential to our feeling of being alive.

People were drawn to Kensington Palace from all over the world. On my first visit, the Sunday morning of the crash, I'd been so intoxicated by the atmosphere that subsequently I could hardly keep away. One of the reasons so many people came is that they understood this unique atmosphere could be captured only by direct experience and never conveyed by pictures or sounds or words (sorry; I'm doing my best). On my second visit the transformation was mind-boggling. It was way beyond anything which could be called a shrine. Bouquets piled high, fluttering with ribbons, glinting with cellophane, flowed like a sea from the Palace gates all the way down to the Kensington Road, and all the surrounding trees and railings were engulfed too. Many perfumes wove about in the air including that of rot. You'd think it impossible for such a multitude of mourners to avoid hack phrases but the originality of the messages was very moving. One I wrote down. 'To Princess Diana. Thank you for treating us like human beings and not criminals. You were one in a million. From David Hayes and all the lads at H. M. Prison Dartmoor'.

On this second visit it was once again a beautiful late summer's day, the whole of London clear and gently burnished. Kensington Palace was radiant in the sunshine. I'd never before observed it so attentively, a great country house in a park, nothing brash, its warm red brick settled in verdure and touched here and there with gold. Though solemn and sad, the mood was the opposite of depressing. It was nourishing and sexual. The drama of Diana's death had invigorated everyone's sense of mortality and this usually arouses the finest eroticism.

On that night of Anna Benn's Russian party, I took Elisa down to counteract the cynicism of the intellectuals, the mediocrity of that response (because even from a strictly sociological point of view these events were gripping). Was this my third visit? I can't remember. Thousands of people of all kinds were sauntering on one of the last balmy nights of summer. Throughout the park, spreading further and further from the palace, points of focus had been created where flowers and candles were placed round tree-trunks, and though electric lamps had been rigged up by the police, there were not so many of them as to ruin the delicacy of the scene. Indeed the throb of the generators provided an undertone to the tremor of candlelight among leaves. Groups of young people made bivouacs, sipping at the atmosphere as at the rarest wine.

Their faces, lit by amber candlelight from beneath, looked suspended in serenity. The scents of flowers came and went, came and went...

At St James's Palace the books of condolence were placed in booths. The booths had to be increased from five to fifteen to forty-three, the maximum number which the rooms could accommodate. I did not go to sign. Joining a long queue to sign my name in a book was not for me. As for the cortège route, it was to have been from St James's Palace to Westminster Abbey, but those in charge were obliged to extend it because of the great numbers expected to line the roadside. The cortège would now leave from Kensington Palace, an altogether more fitting point of departure anyway, which would quadruple the length of its journey. Temporary loos, drinking fountains, and crowd barriers were arriving in the centre of town by the lorryload.

We were all amazed. We were amazed to be amazed but very willing to be amazed. We were all in something very much more amazing than usual. Greek tragedy plus individuality equals Shakespeare. We were all in a Shakespearean tragedy. This was not cinema or television or virtual reality, but actual, visceral reality, and yet like theatre there was something fantastic about it. Between Diana's death and her burial, many films of her were shown on television, moving images of a soul in limbo. It made one think—how very weird it is, this business of being a human being, of being alive. There's not much mystery about death. It's being alive that's the mystery. Death is the normality, life is the exception.

And who was this woman who lay everywhere upon the air like incense? She embodied so many archetypes and was so was rich in contradiction: virgin and ravished virgin, prey and huntress, married mother, single mother, Venus and Jezebel, aristocrat and friend, royal and deposed, rebel and saint, survivor and sacrifice, her life a playground between image and authenticity. Most of this was fortuitous and to my knowledge she destroyed no one, while many, many careers were forged by her death.

Nobody wants a mere saint these days. Like a goddess of Greek mythology, Diana was loved for her failings as well as for her gifts. And she was often hated for the same reasons. Her quest for love was everyone's quest, but her rejection, like all rejections, was hers alone to cope with. After many difficulties, it seemed she was killed on a trajectory that was once again rising. But who knows. Who can say what would've happened to her in life. As it was, her sudden death became a sharp reminder of the temporary state of affairs in which we all live, of the ruthlessness of ultimate truths.

My father, an airman during the Second World War (and who was stationed at Northolt for a while), said 'There's been nothing like this before.' One may ask: would it have been worse if she'd survived the crash as a vegetable? Yes, that would have been much worse. What about survived it but disfigured, would that have been worse too? I don't know. I couldn't say. A disfigured princess can be noble, but can she be magical?

At 8 o'clock on the evening before the funeral, her body was to be brought to Kensington Palace where there would be a vigil with two priests sitting beside the coffin through the night. As the hearse left St James's to drive to Kensington the silence was disturbed only by the flashbulbs of onlookers which made a wondrous flicker in the twilight. It was the ghostliest thing I've ever seen on the BBC ten o'clock news, for all London was transfigured, bathed in an uncanny light. The Promenade Concerts at the Albert Hall continued in full swing of course. My brother and his wife were going to one the next evening. The organisers had changed the first half to Fauré's Requiem but the second half, Rachmaninov's First Symphony, was left unchanged. The premiere of this symphony, in St Petersburg in 1897, had been a fiasco and its ridicule by the musical establishment triggered a nervous breakdown in Rachmaninov. He destroyed the score and wrote nothing for three years. However the orchestral parts were discovered in the St Petersburg Conservatoire after Rachmaninov's death and the music was reconstructed. It is a masterpiece of sadness, with one flaw. I think there has been a mistake in the reconstruction of the last movement in which the soaring main theme, like something from a Hollywood romance of the nineteen-thirties, does not return properly and as a result the work, integrated until this point, ends uncertainly. It is as though a page were missing. Someone should think about restoring that missing page. I tried to join my brother for the performance but there were no tickets left.

My friend Von, the one I'd gone to the Tina Turner concert with, rang and said 'Do you know why people loved her? I can give you one of the reasons. She was the first royal to wear heeled shoes without tights. Gradually she shed her hats and coats and by the time she died she was practically Newcastle upon Tyne on a Friday night. Fabulous.'

London had slowed right down. People were impassioned

but slowed right down. Which are the two best conditions for sex. On September 29th several weeks after all these events, I noted in my journal that I'd had forty sexual partners in the month following Diana's death, including a group of women in a naturist Jacuzzi in Brighton where I'd found myself by chance. Most of the encounters had something accidental about them, and were not coarse or contrived. I'm not bragging. And I'm not going into lots of details. But I've known nothing like it since and it wasn't only me. By definition I was being met halfway. One could hardly venture out of the front door without some interaction taking place in which strangers became friends. It reached an airy culmination off the Portobello Road around 10.30 one morning. I was on my way to buy fruit from Nellie's barrow when a pair of eyes crossed my path, there was the look, I followed him down an alleyway and hey presto, it was all happening screened by packing cases in a little warehouse behind Woolworth's; the whole thing took place in a furtive delirium of, at most, five minutes. Gradually of course everyone relearned the word 'no' after that transcendental, unexpected burst of 'yes'. What remains is that the people who liked Diana were a lot nicer than those who didn't.

On the day of the funeral, September 6th, I awoke spontaneously at 6.15 am. It was a Saturday but didn't feel like one, or like any other day. I had a bath and breakfasted and put on a black suit and my funeral tie. It's the one I always wear for funerals, Yves Saint Laurent from the early 1970s, black with white squares scattered across it. At about half past seven I set out. The streets of Notting Hill were empty. On a Saturday morning,

Notting Hill's most commercial day, the principle day of the Portobello Road market, every shop was closed. There was no traffic either – well, occasionally there was a car. Several people, also wearing black, were walking in the same direction as myself. The sky, as it had been every day since the previous Sunday, was blue and filled with sunshine. What an exceptional week it had been simply from the weather point of view. And everywhere the eeriest calm. The Greeks saw death as blue. Homer writes somewhere about Blue Death. How right they were in so much, those Greeks. The moment you see death as blue its tranquillising wonder is restored.

In Kensington Gardens the activity thickened. If you walk southwards down the Broad Walk from the Bayswater Road – and I now saw that large, quiet crowds were doing so – you can see on your right the backs of the great houses along Kensington Palace Gardens. The noblest mansions of Piccadilly and Park Lane, of Grosvenor Square and Berkeley Square, were pulled down, tragically, only a generation or two ago, but the atmosphere of traditional wealth can still be found in this one road, Kensington Palace Gardens, sublimely redolent of London's imperturbable splendour.

Between the Broad Walk and this romantic vision of richesse is a large fenced paddock where another timeless spectacle could to-day be observed. Horses were being groomed by cavalrymen whose jackets were off and white sleeves rolled up. A dark-green gun carriage, with big spoked wheels, stood on the far side. The flowers, tons and tons of wilting blooms, celebrated across the globe as the greatest ever amount of offered flowers in one place, they were easier to take in now with a sweep of the eyes, since there were no crowds near them, only several figures on the paths gouged through the waist-high mounds, figures who paused every so often to read the messages. I bumped into an old friend, David Jenkins, with his family. We exchanged greetings and observations before walking on independently.

More and more people were crossing the grass towards the Kensington Road and here it was that they crowded, packed either side of the highway, along with officials in uniforms, and the press and television corps. This funeral was to be the biggest media event in history, broadcast live throughout the world. I halted on a damp bank on the parkside of the railings not far from the Kensington Palace exit on to the main highway. Hardly anyone spoke. Such a huge number of people, over a million along the route, each settled into a kind of alert tenderness, created a mood of great nobility, and of something more than that. The previous week had been remarkable but nothing in it had attained to quite this level of...of what? Is it possible to identify what it was? Let me say something like this: I've never before or since felt such a public sense of wonder. What was particularly strange was the peace. It was so peaceful. And safe. In the crowded heart of London town. The one grating sensation was a police helicopter puttering overhead. Its noise faded and returned, faded and returned.

At around 9 am the helicopter began to fade again. But on this occasion it did not return. It continued to fade. With diminishing bursts of propeller noise, brought to us on a slight breeze, it faded away altogether. Putter-putter-putter-put...A few people looked to left and right.

The last scraps of murmured conversation, bereft of any cover, died out. And quite noticeably the silence deepened. It was difficult to imagine that it could, but there was a definite moment when a further, sinking gear-shift took place. Some remaining infraction had been focused and the silence became a vast lake, all-embracing, rippled with apprehension. The birds and dogs of Kensington, being sensitive creatures, picked up on this and were altogether stilled.

The moments passed. We waited. The world waited. Everything waited. Then somewhere behind me and over to the right, a military command was barked out. It was distant but very distinct. After it one expected to hear perhaps the salute of cannon fire, or the jingle of faraway harnesses approaching in a gathering roar. But there was nothing. Except, well, an obscure nervous sense that something somewhere had been set in motion by that single command. The silence became a vortex. Everything was sucked into it. It was peaceful no longer but rigid. It held you and you couldn't move. What was happening? Nothing. Nothing...

Then a wild shriek cut the air. Diana! It was a woman's cry. The whole enormous crowd was electrified and a shudder ran through it. It was ghastly. Primitive. The shudder hit me like a wave and my whole being fizzed up, heart rushed, legs trembled, I was disorientated, frightened, and for a moment thought I might pass out. And there was a second shriek. Women. They were women. A third screamed Diana! And several more. They were like lightning strikes against that profound, terrible silence whose reverence nonetheless held.

What had happened was that the world had had its first glimpse of the object of lamentation prepared for burial as it emerged on to the streets of London. That image would within seconds be familiar everywhere. But for a few moments it was utterly new and very upsetting. Nothing in the comings and goings of the previous week could have prepared one for it, but the women close by had seen it and reacted.

Yet I couldn't see it myself. Everywhere immediately round me was still somehow frozen, tense... Now – yes – something was happening – something moving – a few red plumes and caps jogging in a little group above the heads of the crowd. The frogged jackets and serious faces of mounted hussars. And now, finally, yes, I did see it. That rolling thing.

Such a huge build-up through the week, but when it came, it was so small, and accompanied by so few. But its appearance, flitting between heads in front of me, was mesmerising after those terrible shrieks. The coffin draped in the royal standard, with white wreaths upon it, was being drawn along by the King's Troop on the green gun carriage, the one with the big wheels. It was flanked by twelve Welsh Guardsmen in red who were the pallbearers and on foot. Moving in the lowest of keys and very slowly, this compact group was so weirdly unobtrusive and yet so shockingly beautiful that it became the conduit to something inexplicable. The fingers of my right hand were stuck to my chin. My mouth hung open – yes, this is how it was. In time one loses the intensity of a remarkable experience. One may indeed be embarrassed by exceptional feelings and seek to erase them. So I made notes to counteract that, to adhere to the truth of how it was. Maybe this is what writing is for. So that we can't disown ourselves.

As it passed by, the gentle riffing of harnesses and horses' hooves filled the ears. I began to walk through the park with masses of others, hypnotised by the gun carriage and its burden which sometimes seemed to slide along the tops of people's heads. Those at the roadside could not keep abreast of it because they were jammed to the spot, but those of us in the park could, and I reached the rising ground near the Albert Hall where the view was better. The small cavalcade passed on towards Westminster, jingling quietly through the sea of silence. I walked a little further, paused, and let it go.

It had set off at 9.08 am. This was so that, after a snail's pace march of three and a half miles, the pall-bearers would carry the coffin through the west door of the Abbey as Big Ben struck 11 am. Which is precisely what happened. They were perhaps guided too by the deep tolling of the Abbey's muffled passing-bell, struck once a minute up to the beginning of the service. The effect of this bell, which marked a very large rhythm, was of the greatest solemnity. But as the coffin moved towards the Abbey through the streets of London, past ranks of rapt figures, later on joined by male members of Diana's family, I don't think that the first electrifying moment could be repeated. Bystanders would see it approach and were readied. But when we at Kensington saw it first emerge it was for that instant a dreadful revelation of Death in all its majesty. And those isolated screams from the women enhanced something for us all, something which went to the marrow.

Kensington Gardens had adopted a meadowland policy that year and looking down I saw that my shoes and trousers were soaking wet from dew held by the long grass. So I returned home to change and watch the rest of Di's funeral on television. But at tea-time as I brewed my umpteenth cuppa I could begin to give way to more lateral reflections, and thought to myself, well, I wonder if that is how Cleopatra went two thousand years ago, not to low murmurings of prayer but to occasional hair-raising shrieks from the riverbanks out of a stunned silence, as her funeral barge floated slowly down the Nile from Upper to Lower Egypt, past the already crumbling temples of Luxor and Karnak and Memphis, locations which fell like guillotines behind the precious cargo, slicing away all possibility of return, for there was only now a moving ahead into something else, something unknown and new, as the barge proceeded over the sluggish waves of the delta and floated onward, onward, out to sea...

Acknowledgements

Among the living and the dead, special thanks are due to Bruno Bayley, Rusi Dalal, James Loader, Dolores Maclaine-Clarke, Maruma, Steven Runciman, and Lincoln Townsend; to Jane Davidson for her encouragement and for permission to quote from her and Alastair Graham's letters; to Auberon Waugh for his encouragement and for permission to quote from the work of his father, Evelyn Waugh; to Bishop Crispian Hollis for permission to quote from *Oxford in the Twenties* by his father, Christopher Hollis; to Mrs Brisbane, archivist of Winchester City Council, for assistance with the Bapsy Pavry material; to Peters Fraser & Dunlop on behalf of the Estate of Mervyn Peake for permission to quote briefly from *Titus Groan*; and to David Higham Ltd. and New Directions Publishing Corp. for permission to quote briefly from *Under Milk Wood* by Dylan Thomas.